'VISION ON!'

'VISION ON!'

*Christian Communication through
the Mass Media*

LESLIE TIMMINS

LONDON
THE EPWORTH PRESS

FIRST PUBLISHED IN 1965

© THE EPWORTH PRESS 1965

Book Steward
FRANK H. CUMBERS

Printed in Great Britain
by Bookprint Limited
Kingswood, Surrey

CONTENTS

LIST OF ILLUSTRATIONS

FOREWORD

I HAVE LEARNED over many years to listen to what Leslie Timmins says. He became aware of the extent of the present gulf between the churches and the 'outsider' at the same time and in the same part of South-East London as I did. He has been helping to bridge it ever since. It was then that he saw the central role that religious broadcasting might play in this task. He has taken part in it frequently. He has also thought about it, read about it, and above all watched and listened to it a great deal. So he has a right to speak and to be heard.

One of my colleagues recently wrote that the proper mood of Christian communication is the indicative – not the imperative. Leslie Timmins understands this. He practises it too, as anyone who saw a memorable dialogue between him and Marghanita Laski in 'Meeting Point' may recall.

To enter imaginatively into the real concerns of another person is the necessary first step towards Christian communication. Only then can you meet. Only then, in charity, may a relevant Christian insight be brought to bear.

In trying to play its part in this tremendous work, religious broadcasting needs far more of the stimulus of just that informed sympathy with its aims, and constructive criticism of its achievements, which this book directs towards it. It needed to be written, and it needs to be read by all those concerned, as the sub-title puts it, with Christian communication through the mass media.

KENNETH LAMB
BBC Head of Religious Broadcasting

O VER THE PAST few years religious television programmes have been viewed by millions of people. Some programmes have been competent, a few have had rare and moving quality, and some have been downright ineffective. No one seriously committed to the purpose of religious broadcasting and who has high standards of professional integrity can be complacent about these programmes.

During these same years a small but increasing number of men in all the churches have moved from a critical indifference to a lively appreciation of the possibilities of the television medium within the purposes of God. Leslie Timmins is one of those churchmen who did not require conversion. From early on he has recognized the potential of the medium and has devoted time, thought and practice to its problems.

There are too few thoughtful books in this field and '*Vision On!*' is a most welcome addition. I wish to commend it to people willing to learn the basic background and especially to those prepared to wrestle with the exciting possibilities of television in the service of the Christian Gospel.

It has always seemed clear to me that television does not provide a substitute for the actual life and worship of the churches. It must therefore seek its proper work and I am glad that Mr Timmins sees its end as mission. Responsible religious television ought not to be concerned primarily with building up the faithful. If mission is the aim we should be concerned with men and women who rarely go to church, have never seen bread broken and for whom hymn singing is not bone of their bone and flesh of their flesh. The fact that television aerials grew quickest and thickest in precisely those areas where the churches were weakest and thinnest on the ground reinforces that aim.

Nor is it merely a question of how Christians can use the techniques of the medium to get across a body of verbal belief but what can be said lucidly and with integrity in the kind of relationship which exists between the broadcaster and the viewer.

The questions come thick and fast. If this is our only touch with thousands of human beings throughout the country, are there any better ways to helping the viewer in his surroundings and in his situation consider his relationship to God and to his neighbour? Can those committed to the production of religious programmes find fresh ways of awakening the imagination, the hearts and minds of men so that men may involve themselves passionately and significantly in the life of God's world?

'*Vision On!*' brings us level with the present situation and

provides pointers for those Christians prepared to venture
further and certainly beyond ecclesiastical self-interest so that
religious television can serve God's purpose for the world and
all sorts and conditions of men may learn to live life.

PENRY JONES
Religious Programmes Officer
of the Independent Television Authority

ACKNOWLEDGEMENTS

I SHOULD LIKE to express my indebtedness to a number of people who have given help and advice in the preparation of this book.

Kenneth Lamb, BBC Head of Religious Broadcasting, and Penry Jones, Religious Programmes Officer of the ITA, have given me generous encouragement and offered many facilities at their disposal. Colin James and Kenneth Savidge of the BBC West Region have also shown me great kindness.

I should like to thank Anthony Hoyland and Peter Lillie of TWW, who have made material available to me, as did Guthrie Moir of Associated-Rediffusion, who allowed me to use his research on Last Programmes. R. J. E. Silvey, Head of the Audience Research Department of the BBC, also made available some material used in the Appendices.

My debt to my theological college is increased by the helpful comments made by Kenneth Grayston and Rupert E. Davies, and Eric C. Pigott, Editor of the *Methodist Recorder* gave his expert guidance. Amongst American friends, Leland Case, Editorial Director of the American Methodist Publishing House, and Dr Lee C. Moorehead of St Paul School of Theology have been especially kind.

I should also like to acknowledge my appreciation of the work of Vera Pelley who gave many hours of her leisure time to preparing the typescript and of the care with which Mrs Donald Stoate prepared the Index.

From beginning to end I have valued very greatly the courtesy and goodwill shown by Gordon Wakefield and Frank Cumbers of The Epworth Press.   L.T.

INTRODUCTION

T HE MOST IMPORTANT invention in the field of communication since printing is little more than forty years old, and
the most significant development of that invention is only
twenty-five years old.

Radio and television have changed both the form and the
nature of communication in our time, and the far-reaching
effect of the change is seen clearly when the task of communicating the Christian faith is considered.

When the first religious address went on the air on Christmas
Eve 1922, to be followed in January 1924 by the first broadcast
service from St Martin-in-the-Fields, a revolution had started.
It is difficult for us in these days, when a television set is regarded
as a necessary piece of furniture in most homes, to realize how
young this medium is, and yet how rapidly it has developed. As
with most innovations, it was some time before Churchmen
became reconciled to the idea of broadcast religion. In fact, when
the Dean of Westminster was asked to give permission for the
marriage service of the Duke of York to be broadcast, he refused
on the grounds that 'it would be received in an irreverent manner
and might even be received by persons in public houses with their
hats on'.

Today those persons with their hats on are the coveted mass
audience of the television world, and it is the purpose of this book
to examine the way in which they can be reached in the name of
Christ so that the claims of the Christian faith might be made
intelligible and acceptable to them.

In less than a lifetime we have reached a moment in the
history of Christian communication which is packed with
opportunity. The question in our minds is whether the Church
can adequately use the opportunity, and use the means of mass
communication with integrity and effectiveness.

Ever since the earliest days of broadcasting, religion has had
its place in sound radio programmes. The BBC, a service unique
in the world, has developed its Department of Religious
Broadcasting, staffed by clergy and ministers of the major

denominations along with experienced laymen, and the output through the work of that Department in both sound and vision is carefully planned and executed, and forms a very considerable proportion of programme time. Speaking of its work, Canon Roy Mackay, formerly the Head of BBC Religious Broadcasting has said: 'The main task of the Church today is to bridge the gulf between the Christian understanding of the meaning and purpose of human life and the modern world, whose ethos and outlook are largely determined by scientific and technological achievements which acknowledge no debt to religion. . . .

'In this task religious broadcasting has its part to play. If it is to do this with effect, we must use the resources of radio and television with discernment and skill respecting the autonomy both of the Christian Gospel and of the media through which we seek to communicate it.'

When the Television Bill of 1954 was before Parliament and the introduction of Commercial Television was being discussed, it was decided not to include in the Bill a mandatory requirement that religious programmes should be produced, but the Independent Television Authority was required to appoint an Advisory Committee on matters of a religious nature to be included in their broadcasts.

The Independent Television Authority agreed to arrange for the assistance of the Central Religious Advisory Committee, and now is consulted about its composition before appointments to it are made by the BBC. It provides a main link between the two broadcasting organizations where recommendations can be made matters of major policy. In addition to this central committee, the Independent Companies have appointed a Panel of Religious Advisers and through this panel, which is representative of the major denominations, the day-to-day working of religious programmes on the commercial channel is carried out.

In an address to a Consultation of these Advisors and producers of religious programmes held in Oxford in 1961, Canon Eric Heaton (the Authority's Anglican Adviser) said: 'Religious television has an obligation which it has scarcely begun to take seriously, that of stimulating a much more critical approach towards the medium itself and its unprecedented power to possess the human mind.'

These two brief quotations may serve to show that there is in both BBC and Commercial organizations, a desire to use the mass media with integrity and care, and to try to serve the concern of the Church, as well as the interests of the television companies.

Face to face with the camera and the microphone, the commission of preaching the Gospel becomes at once more difficult, more exciting – if that were possible – and more exacting.

The preacher is subjected to the salutary experience of addressing an audience the members of which can dispose of him and his message at the turn of a switch. He is made aware of the strange paradox that in some ways this is a highly personal medium and in other ways it is the most impersonal form of communication.

He is no longer safe in the pulpit – he is out there, surrounded by technicians, half-blinded by bright lights, faced with technical situations in which he feels a complete amateur, with an audience bigger than his predecessors could have reached in a lifetime.

Or, if he is doing a sound broadcast, he is either alone, or with only one other person in a soundproof studio, finding that he must forget his pulpit voice, with no echoing space around him, and only a winking red eye of light to tell him when to start and when, precisely, to stop – this, in itself, is a severe discipline for most preachers.

He may be in the expert hands of a programme director who knows as much – or more – theology than he does, and has, in addition, long experience of the medium. Or he may be recording six television Epilogues in one morning with a programme director who does not share his faith, knows nothing of the Church, and blandly informs him that the director's job is the technical production of the programme, and he, the nervous parson, is the expert on the religious side – as though there could be a separation of this kind.

It is one of the most urgent tasks facing the Church, therefore, that those who are the Christian communicators of today, should know something of the content of religious broadcasting and television, of the techniques involved, and of the approach to this complex and stimulating method of reaching modern man with Christian information and advocacy. This book is written from some practical experience in the field of mass communication and from a deep interest in the media. It is intended as an attempt to air some of the problems which face us and to discuss the many opportunities it presents. It has no pretension to be a book of instruction. At this time there is a very large 'L' plate firmly attached to most people who have the privilege of sharing in this work. At least we may learn together.

CHAPTER I

THE NEW WORLD OF COMMUNICATION

IN THIS STUDY we are chiefly concerned with the communication of the Gospel to the people who form the great bulk
of the population of this country. They are, properly speaking,
outside the Church. In fact, many Christians have become
accustomed to referring to them as 'outsiders'. This is a curious
and significant description, because it is used by a minority to
describe a majority of people.

The harsh reality of the situation which faces the Church in its
efforts to preach the Gospel has been evaded again and again
by this attitude which many Christians have taken about their
fellow men. In describing them as 'outsiders' they have come to
think that they, the Christians, are the dominant and directive
group in the culture of the country, and therefore anyone who
does not 'belong' is automatically 'outside' the true attitudes
which are representative of all that is best in the life of the
nation.

Although it may be true that the Church – when it is not
institutionally tired out – represents these best values, it is
certainly not true that the Church can claim with any accuracy
that it is either dominant or directive. In fact it is the Christian
with his Gospel who is the 'outsider' in modern society, not the
cheerful non-churchgoer who is on the inside of society, con-
forming to the patterns of behaviour and attitude which are not,
on the whole, those accepted by the churchman.

We frequently quote to each other in the endless conferences
and discussion groups, with which the institutional Church
passes its time, the warnings of theologians like Brunner and
Kraemer. Such men have reminded us that we are in a missionary situation, and that the Gospel continually needs to be trans-
lated into contemporary terms. This is the task which has not
been taken seriously in our generation.

Although the need for such work is emphasized in every

B

conference on evangelism and the outreach of the Church, little or nothing seems to happen.

In spite of a great deal of sincere endeavour on the part of the concerned Christians within the Church, the great mass of people are seldom confronted with the Gospel through the normal work and witness of the Church.

This is not to say that no effort is made. Leaving aside those Christian groups which are either complacent or inhibited by the weakness of their organization – and there are too many such groups, even in the most forward-looking places – there is an awareness that the unreached mass audience is not reached by the usual methods of preaching.

We are reluctant to acknowledge this fact, and when we sit down to consider how more people can be helped to hear what we profoundly believe is the most important message in the world, we often do little more than intensify the efforts which have already failed.

These efforts are based on the assumption that people will come to Church if only we can find a way of persuading them to do so. Then, the Gospel can be presented to them in the context of worship, and communication can take place.

The fact is, however, that in spite of all that is done along these lines, they simply do not come – at any rate not in large numbers. And the indications are that they are not likely to respond to repeated appeals to attend the worship of the Church, however persuasive those appeals may be.

The reluctance of Christians to face this fact springs from memories of the days 'when our church was full'. And many are honestly puzzled as to why those days are gone. The fact that the social and technical revolution of this century has changed the patterns of life almost beyond recognition in a lifetime is one which many people find hard to accept.

Because of the difficulty of this acceptance, most thinking about the communication of the Gospel begins and ends with the idea that it is within the framework of institutional 'evangelism' of one kind or another that people can once again be brought within the sound of the Gospel.

It is for this reason that books which are written for the guidance of the preacher all seem to assume that the young minister, when he leaves his theological college, will spend every morning in his study preparing his sermons for Sunday, and at the beginning of each week, as Sunday dawns, he will ascend the pulpit steps in the face of a crowded and breathless congregation who have assembled to hear what word from the Lord he has for them this week. This seems to be the unspoken assumption behind most books on homiletics, and it results in grave disillusionment for the preacher when he finds that, in the first place, the pressures of a modern ministry deny him the time in the study and, in the second place, the circumstances of the world he enters do not offer him the congregation.

He is far more likely to preach to fewer than a hundred people and most if not all of them have heard the Gospel many times. They have made their initial response in decision, membership of the Church or confirmation and they are not, properly speaking, the object of evangelism.

The present day does not, in fact, offer the preacher the kind of opportunity it once did. In less than a hundred years the situation in this country has undergone a transformation which is not clearly recognized yet.

We still live mentally in the afterglow of the Victorian era, which, with all its weaknesses at least offered the preacher a hearing. Few Christians are ready to accept the hard fact that those days are gone. A picture of these former days may help us to see just how drastic the change has been.

In a book on the Victorian era Amy Cruse says: 'The Victorian age was the age of the preacher and although the sermon was not the only form his preaching took, it was the most obvious and widely popular. No right-minded Victorian thought his Sunday properly spent unless he had heard at least one sermon.[1]'

It was true that only a hundred years ago crowded congregations listened to sermons, and there was a definite public for the preacher. Moreover, the preacher had the ear of the public in more ways than one. The 'platform lecture' was a popular mode of communication and the preacher was very often the man with the opportunity to entertain and instruct.

It is clear enough that the function of the preacher could be one of entertainer as well as one who communicated the Gospel because the Church was also very often the centre of such cultural and entertainment opportunities as were acceptable

to the mass of a middle-class aspiring population, whose
occupations were genteel, but whose preoccupation was
to be respectable.

Miss Cruse points out the fact that not only could sermon
reading and hearing be regarded as a pious exercise, but the
same sort of entertainment could be enjoyed by these activities
as could be obtained from the third-rate novel.

It was this type of sermon which George Eliot attacked in an
article on Dr Cumming: 'Above all, let him (the preacher) set
up as an interpreter of prophecy and rival Moore's Almanack
in the prediction of popular events, tickling the interest of
hearers who are but moderately spiritual by showing how the
Holy Spirit has dictated problems and charades for their benefit,
and how, if they are ingenious enough to solve them, they may
have the Christian graces nourished by learning precisely to
whom they may point as the "horn that had eyes", "the lying
prophet", and "the unclean Spirit" . . . in this way he may gain
a metropolitan pulpit; the avenue to his church will be as the
passage to opera. . . .'[2]

This situation did not, of course, change all at once. For some
time after the period which is so well recalled by Miss Cruse,
there were congregations which gathered to hear the popular
preacher.

As recently as 1935 a book could be published which contained a series of sketches of well-known preachers. It was a
collection of articles which had first appeared in the periodical
Truth, and the author, Muriel Harris, indicated the kind of
congregation which could still be found in the metropolitan
pulpits: 'The morning service at St Martin's begins upon the
pavement. An hour before Dr Shepherd is going to preach, a
congregation assembles under the big portico and trails away
down the steps. . . .'[3]

Even now, of course, this Church in Trafalgar Square is still
full of worshippers, but it is one of a very few metropolitan
pulpits which can be said to attract great numbers. The Westminster Central Hall is another of which Muriel Harris wrote:
'The place is full. No sprinkling here, no effort to make a few
look many. Full, on a hot summer evening, of tidy, well-brushed,
well-burnished people, and in the natural proportions–families,
couples, young men and maidens, elderly men. . . .'[4] They, in

that year, had all gathered to listen to the preaching of the famous Dr Dinsdale Young.

Still, today, they gather in such Churches in the heart of the great cities, but the numbers have grown less with the passing years, and the crowded suburban Churches do not, when they are added to the central congregations which still exist, counterbalance the majority of sparsely-attended places of worship which look accusingly upon the empty Sunday morning streets.

Accurate figures for Church attendance are notoriously difficult to come by – the only official Census of Religious Worship taken in England and Wales was compiled in 1851.[5] Even then, that report pointed out that the 'labouring classes' did not go to Church because, it was suggested, they disliked the class distinction which existed in the Churches, suspected the clergy, and felt the drag of poverty.

At that time, only a hundred and thirteen years ago, almost one person in three of the population was estimated to attend one service a Sunday. Yet when Rowntree and Lavers produced their *English Life and Leisure* which compared Church attendance in York over a period of fifty years, Anglican attendances at all services had dropped to about one in twenty-one.

Throughout the whole period of the past century, it is increasingly clear that the invitation of the Church to come on to the premises and hear the Word has been increasingly ignored, and when it has been accepted, those who have made a response have been largely drawn from the middle-class, or aspiring middle-class elements of the population.

The great bulk of the modern affluent working class have stayed away – and it is a curious commentary on the superficial diagnosis which is made of the situation that, whereas in 1851 concern was expressed at the small number of the 'labouring classes', as they were then called, who were to be found in Church, nowadays affluence is blamed as a principal factor in the situation.

Such observers as Richard Hoggart and Paul Ferris, have painted a picture of the modern Church in England largely out of touch with the great bulk of the community. 'There are a few working class areas in which a substantial proportion of people still attend Church or Chapel,' says Hoggart,[6] and he goes on to describe the frail hold any Church activity or outreach has upon the kind of people who make up the bulk of the working population of this country.

In his book about the Church of England, Paul Ferris, who described himself as an 'outsider', made an assessment of the impact of parish work upon the same section of the population. Despite devoted work on the part of great numbers of faithful parish priests, it was evident to him that little real contact was being made.[7]

There is no lack of evidence that there is a deep sense of this separation between people and Church. The concern expressed by Canon Wickham (now the Bishop of Middleton) of the Sheffield Industrial Mission, and the constant references to the apparent irrelevance of the Church to Industrial Society by those engaged in Industrial work on behalf of the Church, all make the same point.

If 'outside' observers of the work of the Church are aware of this gap, those who are concerned within the Church are also awake to the difficulty of reaching the mass of people with the message of the Christian Gospel.

In 1963 the Methodist Conference received a Report of a Conference Committee on Industrial Evangelism, which had been appointed to survey the work being done on this front.[8] The Luton Industrial Mission under the direction of the Rev. William Gowland had for some ten years attempted to plan methods of reaching industrial workers, and under the Home Mission Department of the Methodist Church various attempts had been made to enter industrial undertakings with the Gospel. Coalfield Missions, such as the experiment in the South Yorkshire Coalfields, had been set up, and some of the openings created by the 'Commando Campaigns' which took place at the end of World War II had been exploited.

It was evident to that Committee, however, that little impression had been made, and that in spite of careful planning and training, no great breakthrough had been possible.

Two years earlier a significant Report had been published by the Birmingham Social Responsibility Project of the Birmingham Council of Churches.[9] This document again underlined the separation of Church and community. Comments from people who were interviewed included this one: 'We don't attend.

Not that we're atheists, but with irregular hours of work it's difficult to find time, and we've lost the habit.'[10]

The fresh approach of this Birmingham survey was that it set out to see how the Church could take its place adequately in the new conditions set up by the Welfare State, but behind the whole project was the realization that the Church was sadly out of touch. When clergy and ministers were interviewed, they were seen to be in difficulties because of the nature of their work and the mobility of the population. They were also aware that they were inhibited by the fact that they were out of touch. 'Most of the men interviewed would have been glad to find a point of entry into the lives of the mass of the people for whom the Church, as an institution, seems to have lost all relevance.'[11]

I have deliberately quoted comments from such varied sources because they all point to the same fact and they come from observers with varying attitudes.

They simply reinforce the frustration which many preachers experience when they face dwindling congregations, convinced that they have been called to preach the Gospel. The problem of the preacher is not only to preach the Gospel effectively but to find a hearing for it. That hearing is not chiefly to be found inside the institutional Church in these days.

Even in the apparently halcyon days of the Victorian preacher, he was still failing to make communication with the great mass of the working population of the country, for they had long before been alienated from the institutional Church in which he preached.

If my argument is sound, and the preacher is unable to meet people with the Gospel within the four walls of his Church, where is he to speak the word? In the eighteenth century John Wesley, confronted with a similar difficulty, took to the open air, and his followers have often done so since, with varying degrees of success.

Except in rare situations, however, even the open-air forum is disappearing. Dr Donald Soper, on Tower Hill and in Hyde Park, still carries on a magnificent ministry in this way. But these are special places, and he is a special kind of speaker in the open air.

For eleven years of my own ministry, in South London and

later on the sea-front at Southsea, I was myself able to conduct worthwhile question and answer open-air meetings. In various places up and down the country, more especially in the summer and at the seaside, it is still possible to make this kind of witness.

Even here, however, the situation is changing rapidly. The difficulties presented by modern city traffic conditions, the reluctance of many police authorities to agree to such meetings and the general apathy of the public all conspire to make open-air meetings less useful than they once were.

There is no doubt in my own mind that a supremely important point of entry into the daily life of the mass of people in this country is the one which is available through the mass media. Radio and television are now part of the way of life of most people in the British Isles, and the world expansion of the media is also a significant development in communication.

It is here that the Gospel may be presented. But if it is to be adequately presented, then the task must be approached with some knowledge of the media, some awareness of the context in which the preacher works as a broadcaster, and some realization that this is a method of communication which attracts an audience with a difference.

It is an audience which is not 'captive' in the sense that a Church congregation is 'captive'. The viewer or the listener can – and often does – annihilate the broadcaster by the flick of a switch. But he will stay tuned in if he thinks that something is being said or done which is worth hearing or watching.

Although the mass media present such an opportunity, the Church has been very slow to realize it. So slow, in fact, that George Wedell, the Secretary of the Independent Television Authority, could say in a recent article: 'The development of the mass media as autonomous organs has been largely proceeded with in the teeth of ecclesiastical opposition and without the benefit of Christian insight . . . the role of the Church has been largely negative rather than positive. It is not surprising, therefore, that with significant exceptions, the institutions governing the mass media have developed largely as secular, not to say secularist bodies.'[12]

This is a biting comment on the way in which the Church has very largely buried its head in the sand as the mass media have developed. The whole purpose of this study of mass communication for Christian purposes is to see whether we can emerge from behind our organized defences and come out into the arena of mass communication, so as to come face to face with the people who listen and watch.

REFERENCES

1 Amy Cruse, *The Victorians and their Reading* (Boston 1961), p. 108
2 Amy Cruse, *The Victorians and their Reading* (Boston 1961), p. 117
3 Muriel Harris, *Pulpits and Preachers* (1935), p. 1
4 Muriel Harris, *Pulpits and Preachers* (1935), p. 112
5 *Census of Religious Worship in England and Wales*, 30 March 1851
6 Hoggart, *The Uses of Literacy*, Penguin, 1957, p. 87
7 Paul Ferris, *The Church of England*, Gollancz, 1962, pp. 20ff.
8 *Methodist Conference Agenda 1963*, p. 123
9 *Responsibility in the Welfare State*, Birmingham Council of Churches, 1961
10 Ibid., p. 56
11 Ibid., p. 13
12 *Frontier*, Autumn 1963, p. 167

CHAPTER 2

PERCEIVING THE LIVING GOD

At the end of his last book, published after his death in 1960 as the Gifford Lectures 1961–2, Dr John Baillie sums up his thesis in these words: 'My main contention throughout has been that we have to do, not with an absent God about whom we have a certain amount of information, but with a God whose living and active presence with us can be perceived by faith in a large variety of human contexts and situations.'[1]

The purpose of this part of our study is, then, to examine the human situation today as it is affected by the mass media, and to see how God can be perceived through those media.

Before we can embark on any consideration of techniques and methods of presentation in religious broadcasting and television, there is a prior task. It is to ask some fundamental questions about precisely what is being attempted.

If it is true that the living God can be perceived in the context of television and radio, then the Christian communicator has to seek the answer to some basic questions before he can properly begin his work.

And the first of these questions is fundamental to the whole of his approach. It is this: Can a medium which is generally regarded as being for the purpose of entertainment be the means by which the Christian Gospel is mediated?

Not everyone, of course, would agree that television and radio are to be regarded merely as a media of entertainment. We may prefer to call it a medium of diversion and maintain that by the proper use of programme schedules and methods of integrating programmes, thoughtful and stimulating features can be sandwiched in between light periods of entertainment. In this way the viewer and listener can be helped to an appreciation of the more serious types of programme, and become involved in them.

If, however, television and radio are easily recognized as media of diversion or entertainment, they are also obviously good media of education and instruction.

The point was made by Sir Gerald Beadle in his recent book when he said: 'Educational broadcasting to me means broadcasting which is informative or which stimulates thought or which develops latent tastes for good art of all kinds; it is the kind of broadcasting which broadens people's mental horizons, encourages a proper sense of values and enhances wisdom. It is a positive approach to people as distinct from pure entertainment, which aims to amuse and relax without making any demands on their minds.'[2]

Can broadcasting be used to carry the viewer or listener a stage further? Sir Gerald Beadle has come near, but not near enough, to defining the function of religious broadcasting.

The Christian communicator will want to do all the things he mentions, but in addition to such a positive approach, he will seek to obtain a positive response and a clear commitment from the viewer and listener.

Some Christian broadcasting will, of course, be educational in a proper sense, and also instructive. But beyond the programme which seeks simply to inform or enlighten, will be the programme which seeks to convince.

Christian broadcasting will, in fact, seek to involve people in a decision about Jesus Christ. But before that can happen, there may be a great deal of ground to cover. Christian apologetics will find a place – and a much more important place – in programming. The presentation of the Christian faith will need to be delivered from the jargon and woolliness of thinking which characterizes so much of it. It will have to be seen as something more than a merely personal matter.

The Christian broadcaster who seeks for a commitment from his audience is asking them to do something which is intensely personal, but he must also help them to see that their personal decision or commitment will have considerable social consequences.

All this has to be done in the context of 'Coronation Street' and 'Z Cars' with all the competition such programmes provide in terms of the viewing audience.

There is a dilemma for the Christian broadcaster in the situation, because he is not offering an easy cure-all but a way of life. And that way of life is not to be fictionalized or made more palatable simply to attract an audience.

Yet at the same time, if he is to be realistic, he will understand that he needs to use television and radio terms in such a way as to keep his audience while he helps them to see that what he has to say is important and relevant.

This will mean that a great deal of the programme time which is available will be used for the direct preaching of the Gospel in terms which will be suitable much more for the non-churchgoer than for the orthodox believer.

As George Wedell says: 'In the field of programmes the objectives which Christians should stand for are not necessarily those most likely to benefit the immediate interests of the ecclesiastical organizations. They will be concerned to see that programmes are lively and interesting. Without these qualities they will have no audience. They will also, however, be concerned to see that programmes reflect life as it is, in all its harsh counterpoint of love and hate, order and violence, courage and cowardice. They will shrink less from the four-letter word in context than from a vacuous soap-opera without any relevance to real life. And they will be more concerned to show the worth of truth and charity and sacrifice than to pretend that these qualities inevitably win the day for those who practise them.'[3]

I have quoted this comment at length because it comes, not from a parson but from one who is professionally involved in the commercial world of television.

I do not see it as an appeal for 'kitchen-sink' religion, but as a plea for the kind of realism which is achievable in television and radio for the sake of Christian truth.

The depression of the preacher's position referred to in Chapter 1 has brought with it a lowering of realism within the framework of 'normal' preaching. When the satirical revue 'Beyond the Fringe' produced its famous 'sermon', the whole thing was a little too near the truth to be comfortable. If you have a congregation who cannot, at least out of mere politeness, move until the sermon is finished, and you are preaching in a context of inaction, as many preachers find themselves forced to do, there is a danger that platitudes will do.

Any regular worshipper could make a 'sermon' which contains many of the words and phrases which he hears Sunday by Sunday and at the end of the exercise find that he has said precisely nothing.

The most fearful results have followed. If a preacher by any chance tries to say something, he is accused very often of departing from the safe and irrelevant by-paths of 'devotional' preaching, and told that he must not deal with 'real' issues like politics and economics and sex in the pulpit.

Yet the love and hate, the courage and cowardice and the order and violence which make up our world are seen more clearly than anywhere else in the Crucifixion of Jesus Christ. And if the message of the Resurrection victory over hate, violence and cowardice and death is to be preached, it must be delivered in ways in which people recognize that these are matters of life and death in the sixties.

People unaccustomed to Biblical language, unversed in 'religious' terminology will, however, need to see such a message in terms which they can understand. We must accept the discipline of beginning where they are, not where we want them to be.

Is this possible? I believe it is, although until now it has been done only in a limited and exploratory way. This is chiefly because there is still insufficient trust between the Church and professional television technicians and producers.

There is blame on both sides here, but the Church needs to admit its own responsibility in this matter. There has been a suspicion and hostility about broadcasting and television from many churchmen and congregations.

When television became almost universal, it was made a new whipping-boy when complaints were made that people were being kept from Church by their addiction to the small screen. It was partly this kind of pressure which brought into being the 'Closed Period', that blank in early Sunday evening viewing which has been filled now by religious broadcasting.

One is tempted to reflect that if Christians had so tenuous a hold on their faith and so little need of worship that television programmes could keep them away from the means of grace, perhaps it was as well that both they and their Churches realized that this was the case.

The curious result of the Closed Period – about which I will say more in a later chapter – was that a major part of television religion was put out at a time when some of those who should be most concerned about quality were debarred from seeing the programmes if they went to an evening service in Church. This produced another tension, and it also produced a great deal of completely uninformed criticism of the 'I was told that somebody on Meeting Point said . . .' variety.

Now that the BBC have replaced the Epilogue with a repeat of 'Meeting Point', at least it is possible for Christians to see Christian programmes on Sunday and this should have some effect upon both the Christians and the programmes.

Given the kind of trust in one another which is necessary between the Church and professional television staffs, some excellent programmes have been produced which put into contemporary terms the incisive quality of the Gospel.

To some extent, at least, the dilemma of producing Christian realism in a medium which is so often obsessed by commercial and entertainment value has been met through the medium of religious drama. 'About Religion' was the first regular weekly television programme about Christianity. It was put out by ATV and its declared intention was to make religious news. In a book with the same title, Michael Redington, its producer, has reproduced some of the scripts which have been used in this programme, and in an Introduction he says: 'It is idle to deny the opportunity that television offers the Church, but it is equally idle to deny that the Church is still at a loss to know how to make contact with and project its reality to this vast new mass audience. . . . One thing is certain: however it sets about the task it can no longer *automatically* assume that its main concern is to 'fill the pews on Sunday'. It must be prepared to shape new solutions as it gets to know and understand new needs.

'Nor is the task made easier, in mass-entertainment terms, by the story that the Christian Church has to teach. It is not a success story in any sense that can be casually appreciated . . . it forces men to see the truth of the situation that surrounds them and to examine it in the light of their relationship with God.'[4]

This imaginative and sensitive professional has again put his finger unerringly on the tender spot. The tension of the Christian broadcaster is the tension of one who believes that he has a meaningful message for the whole of the audience he is potentially able to reach, yet who is aware that very often what he has to say is difficult to state and unpalatable to the hearer, or viewer. Perhaps the only way in which this can be done at all is by the establishment of confidence between the broadcaster, producer and audience.

It is very easy to underestimate the perception of the mass audience. If the viewer comes to recognize that a given programme is trying to face the difficulties inherent in the programme with honesty, and if he sees that there is integrity in both production and performance, then the beginnings of a relationship may be made between viewer and programme, and the content of the programme can be varied so that the Christian truth emerges in different forms but with consistent emphasis.

'Success' in the purely commercial sense will not be the yardstick, then, of the Christian broadcaster. He will do everything he can to win and keep his audience, but he will never sacrifice his integrity to his programme ratings. He will always remember that behind the camera and the screen and the microphone lies the living Church in the community. But he will not try to make his broadcasting a means of filling his pews. His primary concern will be to speak the truth as incisively and compellingly as he can, in picture, drama, or speech and offer his work to God to be used for His will.

What, then, are our criteria for the use of these media?

The most popular reply to that question I have met is that the Christian broadcaster must be 'sincere'. But we might well ask 'what is sincerity?' We have sometimes been told that the television camera cannot lie about a man's sincerity; that it is a penetrating instrument which exposes insincerity at once.

It is certain that many people regard it as a high compliment when they are told that they are sincere, and yet it seems a poor tribute to say that a man who is trying to proclaim a faith which, he would claim, means life itself to him, is 'sincere'!

Certainly, the word has lost its value to some extent nowadays. Malcolm Boyd has pointed out that Frederic Wakeman in his novel *The Hucksters* spoke of a man wearing 'a sincere tie'! and talks at some length of the virtues of the unaggressive performer.[5] But he also rightly asks how does the institution of the Church cultivate such a trade-mark? This question is particularly relevant when one remembers the antipathy toward the Church

1. Methodist Ministers attend Religious Training Course. In this picture taken in the studios are, left to right, Revs Leslie Timmins, Leslie Goy, Kenneth Greet, J. M. Neilson, Vincent Parkin and John Jackson.

2. Mr Penry Jones, Religious Adviser to ITA, talks in ABC Television Studios to the Rev. Arthur Shaw and the Rev. Leslie Timmins.

which is real enough even when it is expressed in cheerfully cynical terms.[6]

Perhaps we can take it then as a *sine qua non* that we need sincerity, or certainly integrity in the presentation of the message.

But it is just at this point that we find it most difficult. The television performer, particularly if he is a parson, may find it very difficult to keep faith with his audience and, at the same time, find favour with his professional critics, especially those who are to be found in the Church. He is open to the temptation to please the intellectual, and lose his touch with the mass audience, who are not really interested in abstractions. His training will not help him here, for if he has studied philosophy and theology, he will be at home in abstract terminology, and – occasionally – too anxious to win approval from his friends and intellectual acquaintances.

REFERENCES

[1] John Baillie, *The Sense of the Presence of God*, 1963, p. 261
[2] Gerald Beadle, *Television: A Critical Review*, 1963, p. 93
[3] George Wedell, *The Church on the Air*, art. in *Frontier*, August 1963, p. 171
[4] Michael Redington (ed.), *About Religion*, 1963, pp. 14–15
[5] Malcolm Boyd, *Crisis in Communication*, 1957, pp. 38–9
[6] E.g. see R. Hoggart, *Uses of Literacy*, pp. 88, 231

CHAPTER 3

GOD IN RELATIONSHIP TO MAN

The Divine Event and Pseudo Events

'THE PROCLAMATION of the Gospel is, in my view, the part of the Christian ministry to which broadcasting is pre-eminently suited and for which "religious time" should be mainly used.' In the words of a commission on broadcasting of the United Church of Canada, the Church exists to proclaim 'the good news that God has come to share our human lot in the life, death and resurrection of Christ for the purpose of redemption and reconciliation. *This is the Word, without reference to which no other fact or concern of life can be properly understood.*'

'But how can this proclamation be made in such a way that it goes home?'[1]

This assertion, that the objective of the Christian communicator in the mass medium is the presentation of the Gospel, is one which we need to take more seriously than we do. At present there is danger that in Christian broadcasting we are too unsure of the objective.

There is, of course, a place, and a proper place, for what might be called 'pastoral broadcasting'. This is the kind of service which can be provided for the Christian who is prevented from normal participation in worship, the people who are housebound or for other reasons find it difficult to be actively part of the Church in its formal setting.

Pastoral broadcasting can also give instruction and offer discussion which is often missing from the life of the local Church, and it can give Christians an opportunity to overhear Christian minds at work on a wide front of ideas. All this is necessary and good.

But the bulk of listeners and viewers are not sufficiently committed to the Christian faith to be active members of the Church. And it is to them that the religious broadcaster must speak. In a proper sense the proclamation of the Gospel is the business of the broadcaster – for he has an audience available to him which is composed of a great variety of people who are not reached at all by the normal activities of the institutional Church.

The 'good news' must in fact be announced as news which is as relevant as the activities of the news-makers in the world, so that 'The Word' – the declaration of God's great acts in Jesus Christ – must be heard as the Word which interprets every other word which is spoken.

When Mr Wedell asks how this proclamation can be made in such a way that it goes home to the hearts and minds of the listeners, he poses the key question of Christian communication and in considering it we are at once confronted by a sharp contrast which is provided by the very media we seek to use.

Christians see in the Divine Event which is the Incarnation of Christ, the ultimate reality, which, when it touches life, makes all life real.

The difficulty is this: the 'reality' which is so clear to the Christian is regarded as an unreality by many people who hear him talk about it. Christianity is put into a 'fairy tale' category, so that it is not merely regarded as irrelevant, impossibly idealistic, and 'all right if you happen to be religious', but is considered not to belong to the 'real' world at all.

This attitude has infected the Christian's thinking to such a degree that it can be detected in much of the thinking which is done by Church members themselves. For many churchgoers, the Sunday service is the whole of their Christian activity, and even this has become dissociated from their 'ordinary' lives, so that they speak of 'going back to the world on Monday'. It is as though they can conceive of themselves shutting the door for worship so that the 'real' world can be left behind for an hour.

The fact is, as Hendrik Kraemer has pointed out, that the Christian world has become 'enchanted' by secularized thinking. And disenchantment must take place on a deep level, within Christian institutions, if there is to be any communication of the Gospel.

The communication of the Gospel has become complex partly because of this infection of the Church by secular attitudes. The Church cannot keep itself to itself – although in too many ways it has tried to do this. And this creeping secularization of thought has reduced its confidence in the Divine Event as an interpretation of life.

For too long the recital of the Gospel has taken place within the context of an 'in-group' at worship, when the hearers were familiar – perhaps too familiar – with both the content of the message and the terminology in which it was being delivered.

Alongside this, the secularization of the minds of the hearers has been so complete that they have begun to share – albeit unconsciously – the scepticism of the unbeliever about the power and meaning the Gospel can have.

The result has been that when opportunities for declaring the Divine Event in the non-religious context of the mass media have come, the same terminology has been used, and this has been meaningless to an audience which is theologically illiterate. And the same nervelessness has pervaded the declaration. Often the only thing that has been communicated has been an uncertain and apologetic suggestion that God might, after all, be interested in the men He has made. That the men He has made have proved to be totally uninterested in Him is not surprising.

So, from the 'in-group' standpoint the Divine Event has been reduced to an over-familiar recitation of well-worn religious remarks, couched in suitable 'evangelistic' terms which were not in fact evangelistic, because they have been addressed in the main to the converted. When the 'in-group' has attempted to reach those people they refer to so significantly as 'outsiders', the same tiredness has been evident in the communication and the result has been breakdown.

Modern man has become inaccessible to the Gospel and the attempt to communicate it must therefore begin from the beginning. As Malcolm Boyd has reminded us: 'We are not to envisage a Christian people to whom we are speaking a message of reminder about a message they know. St Paul in Acts 17 gave his talk to the Athenian philosophers. The philosophers heard and refused; but at least they had met, at least they had heard. We must enable the Gospel to be *heard* today.'[2]

The presentation of the Divine Event to the man who is on the outside of the institutionalized Church is complicated by another factor. It has to do with our change of thinking about the nature of Man. The Gospel is essentially a statement about Man, and his relationship with God. If our beliefs about man change radically, then our attitude about the nature of his relationship with God will change. And this has happened.

To illustrate this change I quote from a non-theological comment on the human situation by Daniel J. Boorstin. He says: 'One of the oldest of man's visions was the flash of divinity in the great man. He seemed to appear for reasons that men do not understand, and the secret of his greatness was God's secret. His generation thanked God for him, as for the rain, or the Grand Canyon or the Matterhorn, or for being saved from wreck at sea. . . . Two centuries ago, when a great man appeared, people looked for God's purpose in him; today we look for his press agent. Shakespeare in the familiar lines, divided great men into three classes, those born great, those who achieve greatness, and those who have greatness thrust upon them. It never occurred to him to mention those who hire public relations experts and press secretaries to make themselves look great.'[3]

So, argues Boorstin, the hero becomes the celebrity and the pseudo-man is born. This pseudo-man responds in the main to the pseudo-event. We live in a world of pseudo-events and this type of synthetic history-making is the subject of an interesting chapter in the same book.[4]

'The intriguing feature of the modern situation however comes from the fact that the modern newspapers are not God. The news they make happen, the events they create, are somehow not quite real. There remains a tantalizing difference between man-made and God-made events.'[5]

Into this world of pseudo-events, peopled by pseudo-heroes comes the Christian with his Divine Event. He has to make reality out of this situation and he has no liberty to play with the facts.

This is the tension of the Christian communicator, for his task is to help modern man to recognize his actual condition, which is that of a sinner who is estranged from the reality which is God. It is this estrangement which caused the estrangement from other individuals and it is only the God who acts in the Divine Events who can offer reconciliation.

Unless the breakthrough can be made, man, denying his true nature, as a child of God, will not only continue to be a sinful creature but will continue to withstand the redemptive work of Christ, seen in the Divine Event.

This means that the task of communication is in the first place the task of helping one another to face the unpalatable truths. The man outside the Church will not enjoy being told that he is a pseudo-man, involved for most of his life in pseudo-events, even though they may range from interviews with people who merely talk about the news but never make the news, to the latest 'Detergent Event' which has no reality at all outside the minds of those who wish to sell more detergent.

The man inside the Church will certainly not enjoy being told that his religion is often infected with the same kind of pseudo-event thinking, and that 'evangelism' or 'Gospel meetings' are not likely to have much reality if all 'evangelism' is conducted within the world of the religious 'pseudo-event' where the offer of the Gospel is repeated *ad nauseum* to people who may normally be presumed to have accepted it already, and who are not likely to make any real response, either because they inwardly long for knowledge of what their next step should be, or they only seek a mere repetition of the 'blessedness that once they knew' when no repetition in such terms is possible.

When the 'pseudo-man' created by an astute publicity and press service and the pseudo-religious man created by an inward-looking Church come together in the search for reality which will deliver them both from the falsity in which they are both imprisoned, there may be a chance for the Divine Event to have an impact upon the real man, and something true and life-changing may then take place in both the Church and the secular society.

That this task is difficult in the extreme is realized by those who are most closely concerned in attempting it. Michael Redington, who has presented imaginative and sometimes brilliant productions in 'About Religion', has commented on it in a publication which is mainly a collection of scripts from that series, in the passage I have quoted in Chapter 2 (see page 19).

Such a realistic presentation of the Gospel to the audience is, however, only possible when the Church is willing to come out of the world of cliché and religious jargon, into the potent and sometimes jarring world of drama and documentary of the kind that has been attempted in some of the programmes such producers as Redington have given us.

And it is all too plain that the cry goes up from such men

that Christians are reluctant to participate freely in experiments.

Perhaps it is because we have been too long locked up in the relatively safe world of institutional religion, where the moth could safely feed undisturbed and the rust corrode our domesticated Gospel. To venture into this may be to seek the kind of martyrdom Christians once experienced in another kind of arena in ancient Rome.

But the New Testament word for 'martyr' gave us our word 'witness', and only as we are willing to expose ourselves to the pain of finding a way through to reality will we begin to make witness to the reality of the Gospel.

Man must thus see himself as a creation of God and make his response through his fellow men to God. In such a response, and perhaps least of all in words but more in action, will Christian communication become possible.

REFERENCES

[1] E. G. Wedell, Secretary I.T.A., in an article 'The Church on the Air', in *Frontier*, Autumn 1963

[2] *Crisis in Communication*, Doubleday and Co., New York 1957, p. 80

[3] D. J. Boorstin, *The Image*, 1963, p. 55

[4] Ibid., pp. 21ff.

[5] Ibid., p. 22

CHAPTER 4

THE REMOVE FROM REALITY

The Nature of Involvement and Fictionalization of the Gospel

IN THE TENSIONS created by the pseudo-world which is one description I have taken to be typical of the problem which faces the Christian communicator, a further difficulty has to be faced. It is that within this framework of 'pseudo-events' there may be a basic unreality about the presentation of the Gospel. This may be true so far as the Church is concerned, and so far as the world to which the Church has to speak is concerned.

This removal from reality lies in the danger of fictionalization of the Gospel by association. If the Gospel has to be presented in a framework which is secular and through a medium which is capable of being used as an escape from reality, the Gospel itself may become fictionalized.

This problem, the fictionalization of the Gospel, is presented to us because of a number of factors which spring from the basic question of how the message of the Divine Drama is to be put across to a people who are unfamiliar with a Scriptural view of life, and who are also in very considerable doubt about the authority of the Christian presuppositions which inform any approach the Christian will make to life.

For the Christian 'The Word' is something full of meaning. The prophets of the Old Testament were always using the phrase in a sense which filled it with action. 'The Word of the Lord' is always for them, and for Christians later, something which is indeed 'living and active and sharper than any two-edged sword'. And the Hebrew word 'dhabar' which was used had a deeper meaning than 'speak'. It had the content of a deed done, an act accomplished.

When God's Word called all existence into being, that Word was effective, and the whole concept was full of action. This meant that when the fourth Gospel began to show how the Word was made flesh, the Logos was again associated with action, and also associated with the whole of Creation in a way that the Greek philosophers could never have considered.[1]

The Word of the Lord, for example when the prophets preface their message by the announcement that the Lord has spoken, is therefore full of action, and the problem is to communicate this sense of the dynamic of God's Word to people without any Biblical presuppositions.

This problem is exacerbated by what has happened in the preaching of the Word within the Church. The authentic Word is made known only when the words of the preacher are filled with meaning through action. The Word is to be spoken but it is also to be lived. And again and again, even where the preaching has been a paramount part of the worship of the Church, this has not happened. Indeed, it might be said that where the preaching has been most central, least has happened, for nothing is more apparent than the development of the habit of listening to preaching and doing nothing about it. The Word is thus misused, spoken in some sort of vacuum, as though it were enough to hear with no imperative need to obey.

Christians, in fact, look like very odd fish to many people because of the curious habit they seem to have developed of 'going to hear a preacher'. When nothing apparently happens as a result of their 'hearing', the man outside the Church asks, in some justifiable bewilderment, why they go, and, above all, why should he respond to their invitation to join them.

A discussion of the way in which the Word of the Lord might become muted and inactive, upon which I have drawn in this chapter, was written by Dr Gordon E. Jackson, Dean of Pittsburg Theological Seminary, in the *Christian Broadcaster*.[2]

Dr Jackson suggests that what he calls 'the Gospel in movement' might be pictured as a series of concentric circles with the Word of God as the centre, the Church as a caring community next, and the Gospel as scandal farthest out and in most direct contact with a radio/television audience.

He does not spare the Church when he comes to consider its place in this scheme: 'Does the Church really care? If so how can it say that it cares through mass communication? My judgement is that the Church itself is a barrier to any communication of the Word because there is too little evidence of this caring in depth. The Church fronts for the Word, and the

Word has so much trouble getting through because the so-called caring community blunts, falsifies, or domesticates the Word. It is in the caring community that the Word becomes visible. When that community does not care, or does not care enough, there is low or even zero visibility.'

Dr Jackson's incisive criticism of the uninvolved Christian community which debilitates the very Word it is supposed to preach may be uncomfortable, but it makes articulate the dilemma we face by allowing the Gospel to become a story to be told rather than a word to be lived. The Christian Church can thus fictionalize the Gospel and remove it from the life which the hearer has to live.

It is this removal on the part of the Church from the real arena of life which is a great barrier to many people who are quite willing to admit our right to go and sing a hymn or two, and listen to a sermon, if that is how we wish to while away an hour, but do not see what it has to do with life and especially with their lives.

Unless the Word resolves itself in action, unless the 'deed' is inherent in the Word, then it seems likely that that Gospel will become fictionalized in the minds of people who listen passively, do nothing and thus have a Word in their midst which, by their own passivity, they have rendered inert.

All this becomes a more severe problem in mass communication because, if it is difficult to involve people by means of a sermon in Church, it is doubly difficult to do so by means of mass communication.

Mass communication is regarded by viewers and listeners as something which is primarily a means of entertainment, or at least a means of diversion. It is perfectly possible to view the most pitiful plight brought to the fireside as news and to reach for another chocolate, have another drink, and say, 'How awful' . . . and do nothing about it.

It is also quite possible that the viewer may watch the most stimulating discussion on the occasion of an election, listen to interviews, comments and controversies, and still decide not to bother to vote. At the same time that viewer can have the comfortable feeling that he is 'with it' and feel an informed person, without the necessity of his becoming involved in any way with the events of which he has been a passive spectator. This may also be true of programmes which set out to involve the viewer in the Word of God.

Two great barriers stand between the Christian communicator and the viewer or listener. One is the fact that the Word is announced every Sunday in Church, and so far as the public is concerned it seems to make little difference to those who hear it. The Church is largely withdrawn from the human situation and full of self-interest – and the man down the street from the regular worshipper knows this, and has written off the Church in any of the thinking he may do about life.

Unless this man is made aware that the Word is spoken by a Church which is willing to become involved at any cost in the life of those whom it seeks to address, he is not likely to respond at all.

Unless that kind of willingness to become involved is made clear, once again we are back to the devaluation of the Gospel which takes place when the Gospel is preached in a vacuum.

The second barrier is inherent in the nature of mass communication. If it is possible to fictionalize the Gospel by merely hearing 'the old, old story' and failing to make any kind of existential response, it is also possible to do so by trying to make the Gospel acceptable by taking from our proclamation anything which might prove to be offensive.

The first business of the Christian commentator is to make common cause with his hearers. It is essential that they should see him as a human being like themselves, confronted by problems, inspired by the exciting business of being alive in the expanding world of today. He is not necessarily using the microphone and the camera to produce glib answers to the problems, or simply to give 'inspirational' comments on the life we live. He will be bound to admit to the tensions he himself is facing, and sometimes he can do no more than try to ask the right questions, rather than pontificate about the answers. Yet he will still claim that his faith will see him through all this, and he will want to communicate the faith which holds him. That faith, however, is faith in God, and not faith in man, until man is redeemed by God and becomes a partner with God in the purpose of God for the world. He is meant to be God's fellow worker (1 Corinthians iii, 9) and unless he realizes that he is made by God and for God he has not realized his true nature.

This realization is the basis of all true optimism about ourselves and the world in which we live, though at first it looks like pessimism. The acceptance of the truth that only utter (and what seems to modern man, humiliating) dependence upon God can bring hope and purpose to man, is the initial demand of the Gospel.

'There is only one firm foundation for any man's present well-being and future hope, namely, that he is the object of God's unceasing love and care. Nay more, that he is somebody for whom Christ died and rose again. And he died to make us not comfortable, nor even happy, but good, yea perfect, which means that ultimately the Christian view of man must be optimistic.'[3]

This utter dependence upon God is the scandal of the Gospel. It comes with unpalatable incisiveness to modern man, whose opinion of himself is pretty good, and who is not in much of a mood to admit to being a sinner in need, much less a miserable sinner in hopeless case without the help of God.

Yet this note cannot be absent from the presentation of the Gospel in order to make it acceptable. As we saw in Chapter 3, if we do omit the pain and tragedy of the Gospel we debilitate it, and this may be done with the best of intentions. Mary Crozier, pointing out the dangers of what she calls 'amiable bouts of shadow boxing', goes on to say:

'Christianity is strange, paradoxical (it always has been), hard and exciting. It is not obvious or comfortable and the questions of the doubter or the unbeliever will have to be answered with doctrine.'[4]

And there cannot be any doubt about the basic challenge inherent in the doctrine. However we may long to take with us the coveted mass audience, it will be necessary for the hard facts of the Christian life to be honestly presented.

But perhaps a generation which is ready at some levels at least to listen to the hard sayings of modern dramatists like the Frenchman Sartre and the Englishman Pinter may be more willing than we suspect to give a hearing to the Gospel when it is shown to be part of the pain and triumph of life itself. This will mean, as I believe, that 'religious' television will have to come out of its religious 'ghetto' in specialized slots in the schedules, and this is the subject of the next section of our study.

REFERENCES

[1] For a discussion of how the Fourth Gospel uses the Logos in a Hebraic sense, see Alan Richardson, *An Introduction to the Theology of the New Testament*, Harper, New York, 1958

[2] Gordon E. Jackson, 'Theological Basis for Evaluation Critique in the Use of Radio and Television', *Christian Broadcaster*, April 1963

[3] Eric Baker, *The Faith of a Methodist*, 1958, p. 61

[4] Mary Crozier, *Broadcasting*, 1958, p. 182

CHAPTER 5

DECISION-MAKING AND PERSUASION

IF WE CONTINUE to think about what constitutes 'success' in Christian communication in the mass media, we are brought up against another related problem, that of persuasion and decision-making. Any attempt to communicate the Gospel is the attempt to convince the hearer that the Christian way of life is the way of life to be followed, and that the Christian Gospel is to be accepted. As has been stressed again and again, the preacher is a herald announcing the good news that God in Christ is offering a choice to man. That choice is a matter of life and death, and the way of life is acceptance of the Gospel.

No Christian broadcaster, therefore, can do his work in a way which isolates the content of his message from the necessity of decision about the message. He wants a decision. He seeks to persuade.

It is true, of course, that he will try to present the message of the Christian faith as cogently and attractively as possible. He will try to find ways in which it will appear as reasonable and sensible. He will make common cause with his audience, and begin where they are, in order to get them where he wants them to be. But he is in no doubt about where that is. It is the point of decision. As Edward Rogers reminds us: 'There were three crosses raised on the hill of Calvary on Good Friday, three cross-beams crimsoned with the blood of pierced hands. If I look and sympathize and sorrow and turn away, they are three crosses only. But if I open my heart and mind to the truth, and know by faith who it is that stays bound by love alone to that central Cross and why He hangs there, then reconciled to God and stirred by Him to the first intimations of immortality, I begin at last and for ever to live.'[1]

Unless men open their minds and hearts to the truth of the faith, and share that faith, the efforts to use the techniques of mass communication have, in the end, failed. This, the unspoken assumption behind every radio and television programme labelled 'religious', is, however, an assumption which leads us into a tension which grows more intense all the time.

In the mass media we are involved in the mass-persuasion techniques we are using. The religious programme takes its place in a schedule which will include other programmes which have a persuasive function. Even though at the moment the 'insulation period' which is supposed to divorce religious programmes from commercials, separates in a nominal way, the broadcasting of religious ideas from the soap opera, it is still true that the Christian broadcaster is working in the context of other kinds of persuasion. This seems more obvious in the commercial television field, but it is equally true in BBC programmes, in different ways – for example when Christian broadcasting stands near political party programmes.

In any case, it seems certain that the 'insulation period' will go before very long, and many people think this would be a realistic move. So there are paradoxical elements present in the attempt to communicate Christianity in a medium which is capable of exploitation.

The point is well made by Malcolm Boyd when he poses a number of questions about the place of religion in this world of persuasion and exploitation. 'We must ask ourselves some hard questions,' says Boyd. 'Is our task that of exploiting bodies and minds by sword, and pen, guns and films for this Lord who became weak and emptied Himself for our sakes; or is our task that of surrendering sword and pen, guns and films, to Him, and emptying ourselves, so that He may work through our "empty-ness" –which is, in fact, a necessary act of surrender before the triumph in us of His grace? When does evangelism become exploitation? Is the Church free to "exploit" for Jesus Christ and for the Kingdom of God? When is a "technique" (even a "religious" technique) *really* religious – indeed, Christian – and when is it not? The answers arrived at, amidst all the publicity and bigness of the climate in which we live, might well confront us with a cross-roads in our mass evangelistic task.'[2] This insistence upon decision is one which pervades all the thinking we must do about mass communication. For, as Paul Tillich has pointed out, the Christian Gospel is not merely for consent but for definite decision. The reason for communicating the

Gospel is so that people can decide for or against it.[3] Christian communication, therefore, is to be undertaken in order that decision becomes possible. Free decision-making must be part of the response to the programme. Reason will, of course, be involved, but more than reason will be in the situation because all kinds of emotional responses might also be present. And the moment we realize that, we are compelled to remember that exploitation and manipulative techniques are not permissible to the Christian, because these would deny everything that he believes about the autonomous nature of man.

We need to pause here, however, and think about how much influence is actually wielded by the persuaders. Can radio and television actually be the means by which people are persuaded to change their whole attitude to life and God? Is the mass method specifically suitable for this purpose? Such popular writers as Vance Packard in books like *The Hidden Persuaders* and *The Status Seekers* have made a case for mass persuasion.

There is a danger of accepting too easily the fact that persuasion can be guaranteed if only the right methods are used, and an equal and opposite danger of being terrified of using mass communication because we mistakenly think that we are to be involved in a monster of persuasion over which we have no control.

The real problem as I see it for the Christian communicator lies in the fact that in the mass media he is involved in a mode of communication which can be totally secondhand. What Boorstin has called 'the age of contrivance' is upon us. 'We make,' he says, 'we seek, and finally we enjoy, the contrivance of all experience. . . . The artificial has become so commonplace that the natural begins to seem contrived. The natural is the "un-" and the "non-". It is the age of the "unfiltered" cigarette (the filter comes to seem more natural than the tobacco), of the *un*-abridged novel (abridgement is the norm), of the *un*-cut version of the movie. We begin to look on wood as non-synthetic cellulose. All nature, then, is the world of the "*non*-artificial". Fact itself has become "*non*fiction".'[4]

Of all communicators, the Christian has to break through this artificiality into reality. He is offering something which has existential content, and is rooted in the real being of man. If Christianity is the drama of life and death, light and darkness, it is not a drama based on fiction. It is based on fact. And above all the response to that drama is to be in the realm of experience at first-hand.

Certainly, in one sense, the television programme is an indirect confrontation. The very mechanics of the business make it indirect. There is a certain artificiality about a man or a group of men facing television cameras in a studio, and speaking what is meant to be the living Word of God, so that millions of people may hear it miles away. There is no creation of a direct personal relationship, and there are all the barriers of technique.

The participative elements of communication must, it seems, in the final analysis be carried out by agencies beyond the television screen. The Church, the Christian community, must play its part in carrying on where the radio and television programme leaves off. The Christian discussion group, the frontier of religious propaganda and conversion, may have to see its work in relationship to religious programme schedules if there is to be any real extension of the mass communication of the Gospel. If this were the case – and I shall deal with this in a later chapter on the function of the institutional Church in mass communication – then perhaps the broadcaster might be released from the burden of having to do everything himself.

The primary task of the religious programme must then surely be a kind of pre-evangelism, asking the right questions, paving the way toward the right answers. It must be the task of instruction, controversy (of which so far too little has been seen), and the deployment of Christian thought to start people thinking.

Response to the Christian faith can be illustrated, and the work of the living Church can be used to demonstrate what happens when that response is made. But there seems to be a sufficient aim in the work of the Christian broadcaster, when he sees himself as one who is on the frontier of Christian thought and action, where he can come face to face with non-Christian or sub-Christian thought, and allow the light of the living Christ to show the facts so that they speak for themselves.

To those who would object that this is not a sufficiently 'evangelistic' task for the communicator in the mass media, I would reply that so far as 'mass evangelism' is concerned it seems quite evident that most evangelism of this kind is saying too much too soon to its audience. Most of it simply does not get a hearing from the kind of people who are at present watching television programmes, which meet them on their own ground and seek to speak to them in language they can understand. The religious jargon of much 'mass evangelism' is simply not heard by vast numbers of people with whom the Christian broadcaster has a chance.

Here is a field which is unappreciated by the Church in general, and one which may only be available so long as a new kind of realism is shown by the Church.

It is true that religious radio and television audiences can be labelled 'minority' audiences. But it is time that we realized that there are more people hearing something about the Christian faith week by week through the mass media than most institutional religious agencies reach at all.

Furthermore, the impact of the Christian Gospel may well be multiplied far more than we recognize by those so-called 'minority' groups, when they in turn make an impression upon the wider areas of the population. The novelist and publisher, Norman Collins, now Deputy Chairman of Associated Television, emphasizes this when he says: 'The big numbers, the nought parade, may be important. But they are not all-important. For a sense of proportion has been lost when audiences of the size of the entire populations of such countries as Denmark and Switzerland can be regarded as no more than minorities.

'Indeed the word "minority" needs defining, and the whole mythology of minorities calls for closer examination. Not the least important thing to be remembered is that the minorities which Audience Research reveals, are not separate and isolated communities but merely a part, and often a large and always intermingling part, of that same unattainable nought total.'[5]

The Church, itself a minority group in the population in this country, has need to take such a comment with some seriousness. The minority audience programme is not to be despised, for even at its lowest, it represents contact with what may be millions of people. This is an immensely valuable opportunity which needs to be appreciated much more than it is at the moment by the Church, which is often blind to that opportunity.

If there is to be response to the Gospel through the mass media the Church must think again, and quickly, about how it can play its part. At present too much mass communication is done in isolation from the organization of the Church, and in any case much of that organization is only geared to the needs of the 'insiders', so that it is almost impossible to make a major effort to relate what is happening 'on the air' and what is happening (or not happening) in the Church or the parish.

John W. Bachman has emphasized this participative responsibility in these words: 'The Church cannot abdicate her own essential responsibility for the continuing engagement of two-way communication. Instead of replacing other functions of the Church, broadcasting should stimulate and extend them. Unfortunately, the preaching and teaching attitudes of the local congregation are sometimes no better than the mass media in encouraging participation and "feedback".'[6]

There is, in fact, a real danger that religious broadcasting – as well as other kinds of broadcasting – may be conducted in a vacuum. And this will be emphasized if it supposed that it is possible to meet all the demands of the Gospel through the camera and the microphone, isolated from the living Church.

The medium of broadcasting is in fact a medium. The life of the Gospel goes through it, and the true impact of the message is only realized in the arena of life itself, when the viewer or listener gets up from his armchair and gets on with living his life.

This is a judgement, it must be remembered, not only upon the medium of broadcasting but upon the Church itself. If there is no vital religious life and witness behind the screen and the microphone, it is not likely that there will be any vital communication of the Gospel on radio or television.

This fact was put into perspective fifteen years ago in a small book which has been insufficiently noticed. It was written by Harman Grisewood, and in it he said, speaking of the correlation between broadcast items and the activity from which the items are taken: 'A concert or play or a religious service which is broadcast is part of a flourishing activity which continues apart from broadcasting. The world of music, the stage and the religious life of the country have an independent activity. And it is the quality of the vigour which each of these different worlds possess that is more important to society than the fact of broadcasting certain items which may be said to represent them...by habitual listening to the wireless the real world from which the wireless programmes are drawn is apt to recede...if the standard of the wireless programme is high it is so because the standard is high in the various activities upon which the programmes draw. . . .'[7]

The rapid development of the media is underlined by Mr Grisewood's use of the word 'wireless' which has an oddly old-fashioned look to the listener and viewer of the present day. But his point is an extremely important one.

When Christians consider the role of the mass media in helping men and women to come to some sort of decision about the Christian Gospel, they must not forget that any vital presentation of that Gospel is utterly impossible unless it springs in the first place from a vital and concerned and caring Christian community. And that community cannot afford to allow its representatives in television and radio to work in isolation. It must help them in deciding precisely what their role is. It must support the programme, so to speak, 'through the screen' and help to make articulate and definitive the half-formed response which may be made by the most casual viewer or listener.

REFERENCES

1 Edward Rogers, *That they might have Life*, 1958, p. 116

2 Malcolm Boyd, *Crisis in Communication*, New York 1957, p. 44

3 Paul Tillich, *Theology of Culture*, Oxford 1959, p. 201

4 Boorstin, *The Image*, pp. 254–5

5 *T.V. Close-Up*, Spring 1962 (pub. Associated Televison), p. 4

6 J. W. Bachman, *The Church in the World of Radio and Television*, New York 1960, p. 116

7 Harman Grisewood, *Broadcasting and Society*, 1949, p. 77

CHAPTER 6

STANDARDS AND PRESSURES

WE MUST NOW try to apply some of the principles we have outlined to the actual work of producing programmes. In this part of the study, I shall be speaking of the production of television programmes, although much of what I say will, I hope, apply equally to sound broadcasting.

If, as we have seen, it is axiomatic that the Christian communicator will always respect both the autonomy of the medium and the personality of the viewer, he has a fundamental duty. It is the duty of seeking the truth along with the viewer so that this truth becomes vital for both broadcaster and viewer.

He will also respect the job of the producer of the programme, and his team of technical experts, whose job it is to present the programme as a piece of television, or a radio production.

This demand to respect the autonomy of the medium, the personality of the viewer, and the job of the producer leads us to ask the question whether there is any difference between 'secular' mass communication and 'religious' mass communication. And we must answer that question at first by an emphatic 'No'. There is a special danger in regarding 'religious' television and radio as something which is different from any other.

There has been a tendency to look upon religious programmes as those programmes which can only be projected by a protected person in a protected space. The 'Closed Period' idea, which gives some part of Sunday morning and some parts of Sunday evening to religious programmes was arranged in response to the demands of the Churches. Many churchmen themselves now see these as a threat to the relevance of the programmes which are presented under the label of 'religious television'. If all religious broadcasting is going to take place in such protected spaces, then we are in danger of creating a religious ghetto in which it will be increasingly difficult for religion to be shown as something which is part of life itself – and the supremely important part, if we believe in the Incarnation of Jesus Christ.

A further means by which there is danger of removal from reality is the 'Insulation' period of two minutes, which is the present rule in Commercial television. This has been judged necessary to separate religious programmes from the rest of Commercial television schedules, in which programmes are normally preceded and followed by advertising. In practice the only result is that a continuity announcer breaks into the scheduled programme with a few remarks about future programmes, or the weather. The announcer, having served as a 'buffer' between the naughty world of soap operas and the religious programme, then withdraws with a smile to allow religion to be broadcast. This appears to me – and, to my certain knowledge, to many others – to be a false situation. I do not imagine that the continuity announcers enjoy it, although most of them try their best to look as though they do. The thoughtful Christian sees it as one more way to make the faith irrelevant to 'real' life where the real business goes on. In literal fact religion is thus deliberately removed from the modern market-place of the television commercial, and popped kindly into a protected slot where no harm can, presumably, come to it.

There will be an increasing pressure to end this anti-Christian practice, and to let religious programmes take their chance with all other television, and the sooner this happens the better for everybody concerned. If it is suggested that this would be dangerous one is bound to ask: 'Dangerous to whom?'. If religious television has to compete on equal terms with secular television so that all television and all radio is one, as life is all one, nothing but good can come of it. Religious programmes which cannot stand on their own merit do not deserve time on the air in any case, and such programmes which can stand up to competition of this kind will command respect in their own right.

It is a curious thing that at a time when much of the thinking about the nature and the function of the Church has resulted in a longing to break out of the institutional structures in which we find Christianity to be imprisoned, we have allowed ourselves to be imprisoned all over again in a complicated structure of broadcasting schedules. These may give protected spaces for religion but they separate faith from life by implication.

Before the 'Honest to God' controversy broke on an unsuspecting public, Dietrich Bonhoeffer was a name well known to many Christians who were concerned about the imprisonment of the faith within the organization of religious life. His argument that God was only thought of religiously as being on the perimeter of things, seen only beyond the fringe of everyday life, and that He must be found in what we know, and seen at the very centre of life, came as a great new and dynamic statement of what the Incarnation of Christ should mean.[1] His prison letters, written in a situation which was bad enough to send a man mad, have a ring of sanity and realism about them, and his plea, underlined since by many theologians, that we should stop putting God mentally on the side-lines of life is one which has special application to the way in which we need to look at this matter of separated religious television and radio.[2]

The 'Closed Period' will almost certainly be altered with the advent of the second channel of the BBC, and a good thing too. The insulation principle must, in my view, also be abandoned, so that the line drawn between secular and religious programmes disappears. It represents a dangerous attitude of mind on the part of the Church, which always finds a difficulty in preserving the balance between the proper protection of the sacred from profanity, and the improper attempt to keep Christ out of His own world.*

The Christian faith did not begin with a man in a pulpit addressing a captive audience at a time and in a place where he was not likely to have to justify his statements under fire. It began in such places as a carpenter's shop, a small, bleak hill called the place of the skull, a Roman arena with a blood-hungry crowd. In these exposed situations, life was brought to the world by faith, and only in the exposure of that faith in the world of today will Christ still be seen as life and truth and a way for perplexed men to take.

What will this mean in practice?

* While this book has been in preparation, new approaches to the use of the Closed Period are under way.

The Insulation Period is also being dropped for an experimental time of six months, by agreement with the Post Master General. The fact that this kind of change can take place even in the short time that this book has been in the hands of the printer is an indication of how quickly the situation is changing in these days.

First, the Christian preacher who has the privilege of using
the media of television or radio will need to recognize his
relationship with the producers and technicians who are
associated with him in the presentation of programmes. As
many as thirty or forty people may form the team who are
responsible for producing a thirty-minute television programme.
From the programme director, who sits in the control room, after
having consulted perhaps for many hours with those who have
written and planned the script, to the men who work with the
floor manager, the camera teams, the lighting experts, the sound
engineers, the designers, the video technicians, all are part of this
closely-knit team. The people who actually appear on the screen
need to see themselves as team-members also, and they must not
be mentally detached from the technical process which is part
of the production. There is a relationship to be found here which
will ultimately affect the relationship with the audience.[3]

Let us take the producer as embodying this team so far as the
Christian communicator is concerned. He is a man who has
certain pressures upon him, and certain integrities which must
be respected. The producer is, for example, subject to one
pressure which is not always easily recognized by the preacher –
or, for that matter, by the audience he serves. It is the pressure of
the programme schedule. Week after week, the producer of
religious programmes has a slot to fill. And it must be filled on
time. The material available may be good, bad or indifferent.
The ideas may be imaginative or dull. The available performers
will vary in appeal and ability. In spite of all this, on a given day,
at a given time, the floor manager will be counting down and the
illuminated sign on the studio wall will flash 'Vision On',
'Sound On'. The programme will go out and another slot will
have been filled.

In this particular respect exactly the same pressures apply to
'Sunday Break' or 'Meeting Point' as to 'Coronation Street'
or 'Panorama'.

Another pressure is that of the hunger of the mass media.
Radio and television swallow ideas at a terrifying rate. The
parson may, and often does, risk a platitude or a trite idea when
he is facing his congregation on Sunday. And with a certain
kind of good-humoured resignation they let him get away with
it, or at least they give the appearance of doing so. But the trite

and the platitudinous is death to the television programme, or the radio feature. The sheer problem of finding ideas and scripts which are free from platitude or cant is possibly more difficult in the field of religious broadcasting than any other, and the pressure on those who are responsible for the production of programmes is very great in this respect.

If the Christian communicator is going to be realistic in his approach, he will also realize the limitations imposed upon the programme by the budget. I have already referred to the number of people who may be involved in the presentation of a programme. These people have to be paid. Time is money on a studio floor. The cost of making film for insertion into a programme is very high. This medium can swallow money as fast as it can swallow ideas.

This is a factor which is insufficiently realized by some critics of religious programmes. They ask, for example, why we cannot have more religious drama. At least one answer is that there are insufficient ideas and scripts of the right quality available, and insufficient money to allow producers to do more. It is also worth asking whether 'religious drama' as we know it at present will be of service to the Gospel if it is presented. Perhaps if it proves possible to get religious programmes out of the ghetto labelled 'religious television' it will be possible to make more time and money available. But to do that, those who are involved in such programmes will have to produce programmes which can face the challenge of the budget.

We now turn from the pressures which are on the producer to consider the integrity of the producer, which must be matched by the Christian communicator. Anyone who has been in contact with television and radio producers will know that there is a deep sense of dedication to be found in them, and an attitude of integrity about their work which evokes deep respect. When this is added to a professional approach to the job which is shown in all the work they do, the Christian communicator who seeks to be a partner in this work comes to realize that he is seeing something which is to be recognized in the business of communication. The integrity of the medium itself is a real and vital factor. And if he is to be part of the team, the Christian communicator must take the whole context of the medium as seriously as the man whose aim is not specifically religious. Only the most sensitive imagination, the most costly preparation, and the most incisive word and image are good enough. The Christian must ask himself precisely what he means by 'using television'. He must respect the authority of the programme upon which he is engaged. He must go where the truth is leading him, and not try to manipulate the truth to fit his preconceived aim. Much less must he adjust the quality of his message to make it acceptable to the 'Masscult' idea. The Christian who is using mass communication has a grave and far-reaching responsibility to maintain a high standard of integrity in the presentation of truth. In this respect, and perhaps only in this respect, can he be said to have a different task from the secular communicator. It is, in reality, not so much a different task as a more profound responsibility in maintaining the high standard of integrity of programme.

In a thoughtful discussion of the problem of maintaining a self-critical standard of excellence in an ad-mass society, Daniel Jenkins has pointed out the responsibility of such people as pastors, teachers and broadcasters. 'Some of them,' he says, 'assume as a matter of course that modern large scale media of communication are inimical to quality and decide that they must retreat into private life, or as near private life as they can manage. This might be justifiable if culture were a purely private matter. But it is not. . . .

'Others, and these are often in positions of great responsibility in modern society, give the impression that they have no obligation to treat their fellows as capable of excellence and that they are, therefore, free to exploit the weaknesses of mass media communication for their own profit.

'If politicians and businessmen behaved in this way, they would be treated as demagogues or parasites. Indeed, they not infrequently are by those same groups, when it is to their advantage to stand forth as tribunes of the people, or to play the part of Cassandra.

'But in many circles, such conduct is regarded as no more than good journalism or broadcasting, or, in some instances, as good teaching or preaching. It is those who behave in this way, far more than those who wish to control economic affairs in the public interest, who are truly leading their neighbours on the road to serfdom.'[4]

It is easy to see how standards can drop through the use of the mass media when we take a glance at the American scene. In a paper presented to Consultation on the Television-Radio Ministry of the Methodist Church in America for 1964–8, the Rev. Dewayne S. Woodring, Director of the Methodist Commission on Public Relations and Methodist Information, Ohio, said: 'To mention religious broadcasting is to conjure up a vivid multiplicity of impressions. To some the term bears unpalatable connotations evoking funereal organ music, screeching choirs, and tub-thumping, hallelujah-shouting preachers recorded in facilities with the acoustical properties of the Holland Tunnel.

'To others, religious radio broadcasting means a potent force which nourishes religion and extends its outreach . . . where the church may not otherwise intrude.'[5]

We may with typical British smugness congratulate ourselves on not being as those Americans, but it is still possible to have an attitude to the mass communication of religion which is intrusive and un-Christ-like while it avoids the more blatant vulgarity to which Woodring refers. It is the business of the Christian communicator to offer the freedom of Christ which makes men into the truly human beings they were meant to be, to lead them away from the serfdom which the very media he is using may call them into. And he may do this not by offering glib answers so much as by progressively clarifying the questions which ought to be asked, so that he is all the time creating an attitude of honest enquiry. In such a task he will be making a contribution towards the creative activity which best expresses the purpose of pre-evangelism and the communication of personal responsibility in the facing of the truth, which he believes is to be found in the faith he proclaims, and he will be doing this with respect for the authority and integrity of the media he is able to use. How this may be developed within the present organization of the BBC and the ITA will be the subject of the next section of this study.

REFERENCES

1 D. Bonhoeffer, *Letters and Papers from Prison*
2 See also *Soundings*, Ed. A. R. Vidler, 1962, esp. pp. 244–50
3 For a discussion of this relationship see R. T. Brooks, *Person to Person*, Ch. 3, Epworth, 1964
4 Daniel Jenkins, *Equality and Excellence*, SCM Press, 1961, pp. 47–8
5 Presented in Chicago, April 1963

CHAPTER 7

THE TWO APPROACHES

As I HAVE pointed out in the Introduction to this book, the whole life-span of broadcasting is comparatively short – only forty years. During that time, the BBC has had a monopoly until as recently as August 1954, when the Independent Television Authority was created.

Thus, the first experiments and the subsequent developments in religious broadcasting were made under the BBC and the Corporation has in this time been able to create a very considerable organization for this purpose. It has also created a pattern of broadcasting which has been unique in the world.

It will be seen that the approach to the task of religious communication differs to some considerable extent between BBC and ITA, and this is to be expected, because, although the aims remain much the same, the organization is different, and the whole approach is coloured by audience objectives, the difference between a national institution and a commercial undertaking, and variation in experience between the two television channels.

So far as sound broadcasting is concerned, of course, the BBC still has the monopoly, although both BBC and ITA are planning for the future, when, if commercial radio becomes a reality, there will be more concentration on local radio stations, and possibly more radio time available in commercial radio schedules for the religious programme.

Another development is the creation of BBC Channel Two, and the likelihood of a second Commercial Television Channel in the not-so-distant future, and all this additional air-time will mean that more and more programmes will be required, with the voracious demands they will make upon the Church as and when opportunity is given to use time on the air for religious broadcasting.

For the moment, however, the shape of religious broadcasting is plain enough, and one thing emerges very clearly. The Christian Church, although a minority in this country, has a privileged place in the structure of television and radio. The following brief survey of programmes will indicate the very considerable amount of time which is given to religious broadcasting as such, and if reference is made to the Year Books of both the BBC and ITV, it is evident that the programme time during which the faith is propagated is very considerable.

I. THE BBC

'BBC programmes started in November 1922, and the first religious address was broadcast a month later on Christmas Eve. Lord Reith, the first General Manager (as he was then called) of the Corporation then took the initiative, and from 21 January 1923 a religious programme was broadcast every Sunday evening.'[1]

From this beginning, expansion was very rapid, and in 1924 the first Church service was broadcast, the Epilogue was added to the programme in 1926, and eighteen months later the Daily Service was broadcast for the first time.

By 1933 the Religious Broadcasting Department was set up with the Rev. F. A. Iremonger (later Dean of Lichfield) as Director, and he was followed by the Rev. J. W. Welch (1939), the Rev. F. A. House (1947) and Canon Roy McKay (1955). The present Head of Religious Broadcasting – for the first time a layman – is Mr Kenneth Lamb, who was appointed in 1963.

The Department is mainly recruited from the ranks of the clergy and ministers of the Churches, although such men as Kenneth Savidge (West Region), as well as the new Head of the Department, are laymen. Anglican, Free Church and Roman Catholic respresentation is secured, and this specialized staff operate in the Regions as well as from London.

This organization means that producers of religious programmes in the BBC are people with a background of theological training and interest, and are likely to be well informed about the subject matter of the programmes they produce. They are also trained in the use of the media, and are able to work very closely with those who actually appear before the microphone and camera. They implement the policy of the BBC which has

3. 'Carols round the World' (TWW). Children from France, Germany, Spain and Yugoslavia talk to the Rev. Leslie Timmins.

4. 'Men on the Move' (TWW). A discussion on the itinerant ministry. Left to right are Mr Geoffrey Johnson Smith, M.P., the Rev. Leslie Timmins, Mr Douglas Blatherwick and Rev. Dr Eric Baker, Secretary of the Methodist Conference.

become definitive as the years have gone by. The fund of experience in religious broadcasting of every kind has resulted in a clear set of aims and a policy which has produced some very fine work.

The original presupposition of the work of religious broadcasting seems to have been that Britain is a Christian country, and Mary Crozier has summed up the attitude of the Corporation in this way: 'Britain is regarded as a Christian country, and broadcasting has sought to safeguard Christian values and has never suggested that any others should be accepted in their place. This policy has been unchanged, though there have naturally been developments in execution.'[2]

With this basic premise in mind, the aims of the Religious Department are clearly seen as they were outlined by the Rev. Colin James, West Region BBC, in an address to a Clergy School: 'In Religious Broadcasting and television we have two main aims – first, to strengthen and support and minister to those who are fully committed Christians and who are involved in the life and worship of the Church. We also minister to those who by old age, ill health or circumstances are cut off from the active life of their local Church. Second, to try to reach those on the fringe of the Church and those right outside it.'

Programmes which reflect the first aim, that of supporting and strengthening the Christians who are already part of the manifest Church are intended to reflect the life and worship of the Church, and these play a very important part in the output of the Department.

In Sound Radio, the Daily Service is a regular feature which, as we have seen, has a long-standing place in the schedules. On Sundays broadcasts take place from churches and chapels all over the country. For many years what has been called the Main Stream Policy has been followed so that denominational interests are safeguarded. This means, for example, that in thirteen Sundays, seven or eight of these broadcast services will be Anglican, two or three will be Methodist, one will be Baptist, one Congregationalist, and one or two Roman Catholic. In some Regions there is often an Evening Service also, in which case one of the two services of the day will be Anglican.*

* The "Main Stream" policy has thus been taken to mean that religious broadcasting should normally be entrusted to the principal Christian denominations as they are defined by the British Council of Churches.

In addition to the Sunday services, throughout the week there are such sound broadcasts as Cathedral evensong, late-night services and epilogues, and school services. 'Silver Lining' may also be regarded as another 'in-group' type of programme, although its appeal is evidently not limited to those who are an active part of the Christian Church. 'Sunday Half Hour' makes a similar appeal to what Colin James describes as 'an audience of nostalgic religiosity'.

Still in the medium of sound radio, a number of programmes are designed to appeal to those for whom orthodox patterns of worship have little meaning. The People's Service, usually broadcast in a series of four services, aims at a non-churchgoing audience through worship designed differently from the more familiar forms. In other programmes efforts are made to reach the man outside the Church, and 'Lift up Your Hearts' commands a large and mixed audience, as does 'Five to Ten'. The format of these programmes can vary considerably and include controversial matters as well as biography and information about the Church's activity. A recent innovation has been a pastoral broadcast by Church leaders on V.H.F.

All this adds up to an impressive total of sound-radio time, and the output of the Department amounts to approximately nine hours of religious sound-broadcasting a week. When three hours of television programmes are added, something in the order of twelve hours a week of broadcasting in the name of the Christian faith makes a large proportion of time. It is divided roughly into six hours radio and television on Sunday and a further six hours during the week.

In television, the main BBC programme is 'Meeting Point' and this goes out during the Closed Period in the early evening on Sunday. The television Epilogue which used to close the BBC television programmes on Sunday has been replaced by a repeat of 'Meeting Point'. This programme is an attempt to find people, events, situations and problems which are potential meeting points between the Christian faith and the contemporary world. Subjects have ranged from the Denning Report to the 'Honest to God' controversy in the topical range, and such controversial issues as Capital Punishment, Abortion and Nuclear War have also found their place in this programme.

BBC Television also puts out 'Seeing and Believing', which

is normally produced from All Hallows' Church in London and seeks to use a format which combines worship with comment to link together the Church and the world it serves.

'Viewpoint' and 'Late Night Final' (now renamed 'Postscript') both reach the screen in the middle of the week, and these may reach audiences who represent both the Christian and the non-Christian attitude. 'Viewpoint' presents the point of view of a Christian writer, artist or personality, historic or contemporary. 'Late Night Final' is a topical prayer-programme, in which the news is made the subject of late night prayers.[3]

In his relationship to the Producers who work in the Religious Broadcasting Department, what does the Christian communicator find? I can only answer that question from a personal point of view, as one who has had the opportunity of taking part in such programmes, ranging from broadcast services on radio and television to 'Meeting Point' and 'Lift up Your Hearts'.

First, it must be recognized – and this is true for both television and radio, and holds good both in BBC and Commercial Television – that there is an obligation upon the broadcaster to be as competent as he can be. I am not suggesting that we should expect radio and television to produce a group of 'professional' religious television parsons – nothing could be more likely to end in disaster. But I am quite sure that this medium has much to teach us in the sheer hard work of thoughtful preparation, and careful thought about what is demanded of anyone who appears on the television screen or before the microphone.

In this, the producer has an important contribution to make. He knows the medium, the broadcaster may not know it at all. He knows how to get certain effects, and how best to make the point of the programme, and again in these matters the broadcaster is not likely to be as knowledgeable.

I have already stressed the fact that the television or radio broadcast is a team effort. The actual performer must see himself as part of that team long before he appears on the screen, or on the air. There is, however, as I have seen it, a difference between the sort of team he is in, when he works with the BBC and when he works with Commercial Television.

This difference lies in the kind of organization which produces the programmes. In the BBC Religious Broadcasting Department, as I have briefly described it, there is usually the opportunity to plan the programme well ahead, consult about the format, the details of the script, and all the time be aware of the fact that one is working with someone who has been trained in the medium and yet is well informed about the theological background of the subject. This is not to say that there is any form of censorship about the proceedings. The canard that people who broadcast must submit their scripts to the blue pencil of the producer and that restrictions are placed upon what a man wants to say is an insult to broadcasters and the organization of both BBC and ITA. At the same time a producer must see that material is not used which will attack or offend other Christians, and that extreme statements are not made by people who are not expert on the subjects about which they are speaking. Scripts for programmes which require careful timing and complicated camera sequences, must be prepared very carefully, and the producer can also help enormously to rescue broadcasters from the kind of verbal flatulence which seems to be an occupational disease.

In all this there is no suggestion of 'censorship' of any kind, although there seems to be an impression abroad that such a censorship exists. Producers are always, of course, ready to give advice about the phraseology and approach when a performer is preparing the script of a programme. Normally sermons and scripts are seen in advance, but this is necessary both for timing and for checking the script in case of mis-statements which may lead to legal action. There is, however, a very great difference between a producer offering his advice on how a point may be made, and any kind of 'censorship' on the part of the BBC. In my experience no producer or performer would submit to such a thing, and freedom of expression is an essential element of the process of preparing for a programme.

The advantage which is possessed by the BBC is clearly in the long experience which is evident in the Department, and the fact that ample rehearsal time is available for all the programmes. The standard of professionalism from a technical point of view is very high, and the performer is working with people who are 'on his wavelength' in Christian matters.

There is no commercial pressure on the Department, so that audience ratings are not the necessary yardstick by which the programme is measured. On the other hand the members of the Department cannot blissfully ignore the audience, and there is a healthy respect for the fact that there is no point in producing a programme which nobody is going to see or hear.

The dangers of the Department becoming another kind of religious institution are, I believe, very much in the minds of the men who work in it. It would be easy to create a 'Church of the Air' which would reflect the kind of institutional dangers which threaten the institutional Church. When religious broadcasting is one Department of a broadcasting organization which has for a long time held a monopoly of the air and is still regarded as the standard organization, there is always the threat of an 'establishment' attitude which plays safe on controversial issues. The BBC is especially vulnerable in this respect, because there are pressures to which, as a national institution, it is bound to be sensitive.

We have considered the many advantages of the Departmental organization by which religious programmes are produced in the BBC, but the disadvantage of being a national institution is one which can tend to make those who work in it acutely conscious of the 'image' they present. This, in itself, must be a constant challenge to the integrity of the Religious Department, and as they try to find ways in which they can meet the contemporary mind in the name of the Christian faith, they need always to be ready to maintain the freedom of approach which secures the autonomy of the Gospel.

Some of his concerns were expressed to me by the present Head of Religious Broadcasting in the BBC, Mr Kenneth Lamb, and he has kindly allowed me to reproduce them here. He says, speaking of what he calls the essential dilemma of religious broadcasting: 'As my predecessor, Roy McKay, put it, "We have to respect both the autonomy of the Gospel and the autonomy of the media through which we seek to present it." Although religious insights only illuminate if directly related to life, respect for the autonomy of the Gospel demands that we should not judge the success of the presentation in terms of ratings, and of professional and secular critical acclaim. Should this become our sole criterion, we may well end by distorting the Gospel itself – many of the truths of which are not comfortable and popular, but hard and unpalatable.

'The advent of broadcasting will not, of itself, affect the

validity of Chesterton's remark that "Christianity has not been tried and found wanting; it has been found difficult and never tried." It is evident that in some respects the Churches are out of touch with contemporary society through being too traditionally minded and inward-looking. But it is also true that most people today – as through the ages – reject the demands of the Gospel as much because they are unable or unwilling to face them as because the Churches bear inadequate witness to its nature and relevance.

'It is this crucial point, I think, that justifies the existence within the BBC of a separate output Department for "Religious Broadcasting". And it has also led to the present practice whereby the great majority of its members are ordained priests or ministers.

'On the other hand, respect for the autonomy of the media demands that any religious broadcasting must be at least as professionally skilful as any other kind of output. One of my ambitions is never to need to defend a religious programme, or to hear one excused, on the grounds that it is a religious programme. This will not be achieved without skills and resources being devoted to it comparable with those deployed in the general output. It also implies that in the long run religious broadcasting can and should stand on its own feet. It should justify its place in the schedules by the interest and relevance of what it has to offer, both in its own programmes and through the infusion of its own ideas into the whole range of broadcasting. BBC-2 offers us an unrivalled chance to do just this.

'We need the support and sympathetic understanding of the Churches in this endeavour. And for their part the Churches could well take more advantage of the pastoral opportunities opened up for them by the missionary work of religious broadcasting.'

2. ITV

Independent Television, the commercial channel, works in a different way from the BBC. Whereas the BBC is a unified national service, which works on the income received from a proportion of the licence fees which every viewer and listener pays, ITV has as its sole income the revenues from the advertising which is carried by the various contracting companies.

The Independent Television Authority was set up in accordance with the requirements of the Television Act 1954, and the new contracts which have been issued in 1964 conform broadly to the position outlined in the original Act.

ITA, the central controlling authority, builds, owns and operates the television transmitting stations, and contractors who provide the programmes from these stations are selected by ITA. These programme companies pay a rental to ITA which is regulated by the population coverage of the stations they use. The cost of rentals, production of programmes, and the general maintenance of the service they provide is met by the advertising revenue from the 'commercials' they transmit. The ITA is responsible for seeing that the programmes put out by the various companies are in accordance with the Television Act, and is also responsible for the control of advertising.

There is no specific requirement in the Television Act for the transmission of religious programmes in commercial television, and one company, Granada Television, does not undertake specifically 'religious' programmes at all. The Act did, however, provide for a proper balance of programmes and laid down the rule that if religious programmes were transmitted they must be approved by the ITA which in turn must seek the advice of a committee representing the main streams of religious thought in the country.

The Central Religious Advisory Committee was already in existence, acting in an advisory capacity for the BBC in its religious programme output. The ITA arranged for CRAC to serve commercial television in the same way.

In addition to the advice which is available from CRAC, the ITA felt the need for more detailed advice on the day-to-day working of religious programme output, and appointed a Panel of Religious Advisers, six in number, and representative of Anglican, Free Church and Roman communions, as well as the regional interests of Scotland, Wales and Northern Ireland. The programme companies also have their own company advisers on religious programmes who work with the producers of religious programmes at a regional level.

A new departure this year is the appointment of a full-time officer for religious matters in ITA. He is Penry Jones, the former producer of religious programmes for ABC television.

Two consultations have been held for the Religious Advisers of both ITA and the Companies. One was held two years ago at Oxford and an account of this consultation is given in detail in a booklet issued by the ITA.[4]

The later consultation was held in September 1963 at Cambridge when Advisers and Producers from this country and other parts of the world met to share their concerns about the future of religious television.

Religious programmes are presented in two ways by commercial television companies. There are a number of network programmes which are taken by all the companies, and these are originated by one or other of the larger companies.

Then each regional company originates its own Epilogue programme or uses the time allotted in a different way. These programmes may also be taken by other companies on occasion, so that there is a varied output of religious television programmes available (see Appendix II for a list of ITV religious programmes).

The total transmission time on commercial television for religious programmes is approximately three hours a week, although a study of the full output as it is given in Appendix II will show that the aggregate of programme time for religion when all the individual companies have contributed their Epilogue-type closing programmes would be in the region of ten hours over the week.

The main programmes, which are networked, are 'Sunday Break' and 'Living Your Life'. These are transmitted, along with 'About Religion', in the Closed Period, from 6.15 p.m. to 7.25 p.m. on Sundays. They correspond to 'Meeting Point' and 'Songs of Praise' on BBC television in the same period of Sunday evening.

'Sunday Break' is aimed at young people in the age-range 16–25 years. The format is very flexible and includes documentary, discussion, and factual programmes, with a 'pop music' insert. The emphasis is on the life and witness of the Church, and on issues which are of especial interest to young people.

'Living Your Life' is perhaps the nearest comparable programme to 'Meeting Point' on BBC. About half the programmes deal with contemporary talking-points such as race relations, gambling, the Press, marriage problems and industry. The remainder aim to say something about the Christian faith more directly in some kind of teaching format, or a statement is made about aspects of worship or the proclamation of the Gospel.

'About Religion' has sought to deal with significant events in the life of the Church, such as the World Council meetings; it has presented the faith in visual terms, posing questions people are asking the Church to answer. General discussion programmes have also had their place in this format. Michael Redington has discussed the aims of this programme and published sample scripts in a recent book.[5]

In addition to these networked programmes ITV puts out a morning service every Sunday, and this is covered by six of the companies. The remainder of the output on religion is done by the companies in Epilogue form with the exception of those programmes labelled 'Discussion' in the list in Appendix II. More companies, however, are making special programmes on religion and sometimes they will opt out of the networked programmes for this purpose. Amongst the experiments which have been carried out in this way, TWW, the company which serves the West of England and Wales, have done a series of discussion programmes which have gone out in the early afternoon of Sunday and have been repeated late at night in the following week. These have taken many forms, and Anthony Hoyland and Peter Lilley, who are the producers, are seeking to make an impact also with special programmes which so far have been restricted to the Christian festivals, but which may lead the way to integrated television by demonstrating that religious programmes can hold the programme ratings through to the next secular programme – a matter which is very important in the commercial television world.

The Holy Week programmes which have originated from TWW have certainly provided some evidence that it is possible to hold the ratings through religious programme slots.[6]

The audience ratings shown in Appendix III demonstrated the fact that where the religious programme is well presented outside the Closed Period there is a possibility of keeping the audience. The hard fact is that unless religious programmes can do this, no one will really interest themselves in the integration of such programmes. This need not necessarily be a matter of purely commercial interest. If no one is going to watch a programme there is no point in doing it. There is plainly a case for programmes with a minority appeal, but if the mass audience cannot be reached effectively, then one of the principal advantages of the medium is lost to the Christian communicator.

At the Consultation organized by ITA at Cambridge in September 1963 there was a definite feeling on the part of both religious advisers and producers that some part of the present Closed Period on Sunday should be exchanged for a slot on a week-night between, say, 10 p.m. and 11 p.m. at such times as are at present occupied by 'general balance' programmes of one kind or another. If this system were to be implemented, it would provide an opportunity to test the suggestions which have been made that religious programmes could, if they were well presented and backed by a sufficient budget, take their place along with all other television programmes.

The remaining programmes originated by ITV to which I have briefly referred are those which consist of Church services, and the epilogue type of programme. I shall deal with the subject of Church services at some length in the next chapter, but a word might be said here on the subject of the Epilogue.

As we have seen, the BBC has changed its policy with regard to the Epilogue. Until the middle of 1963 an Epilogue ended transmission every Sunday evening on the BBC network. This has now been replaced by a repeat of 'Meeting Point'. In commercial television, however, a considerable part of religious programming consists of the end-of-day type of epilogue programme. Scottish Television puts out a discussion programme at 1.30 p.m. on Sunday afternoon; Ulster Television does a Studio Service at 7 p.m. on Sunday evening; Associated Television does a two-minute Prologue at 12.45 p.m. from Tuesday to Friday (ATV also does an Epilogue); and TWW has exchanged the Epilogue for the discussion programmes described above. With the exception of these programmes all the religious output of the companies is in epilogue form. This, however, must be qualified by a reminder that some of the companies are now experimenting with occasional special programmes, and the network programmes described earlier in some detail fill the Closed Period on Sunday. The fact still remains that, if

TWW's Summing Up programme on Sundays and Thursdays is included, no less than twelve commercial companies are using the epilogue or Prayer-Time format to end their programmes throughout the week. It is important, therefore, to see how this time can best be used. The epilogue is a low-budget type of programme. It can be recorded in advance, although there are considerable advantages in the 'live' epilogue such as ABC Television uses.

The aim of the programme is stated in the present ITA brief. Epilogues 'should be treated as brief devotional periods analogous to evening prayers; whilst providing an opportunity for Christian witness and challenge, they should not be used for controversial discussion'. Members of the Commission on Epilogues at the 1963 ITA Consultation gave considerable time to this question of epilogue presentation, and Guthrie Moir of Associated Rediffusion submitted a survey which had been carried out in the London Area.[7] This indicated that there was reason to believe that a younger age-group is available as potential epilogue viewers than has been thought to be the case. The figures show that in five age-groups ranging from 15 years to 65 years old, the highest percentage of people out of bed at midnight is in the 25–34-year-old category. Admittedly, this is in the London area which may be regarded as a special one, but there is obviously an opportunity here at least to be more varied and perhaps more controversial in approach than the present ITA definition would seem to encourage.*

Further considerations about the epilogue are outlined in a survey carried out by Maxwell Deas of Tyne-Tees Television. Although nearly half of those who replied to a questionnaire which was sent out in his company's area thought the Epilogues were 'good', there was considerable criticism of the title itself, and fears were expressed about emotional and sentimental elements which may be allowed to become part of the programme.

The need for great care in the use of the opportunity offered by the Epilogue was emphasized by the replies: 'Criticism is levelled at the platitudinous Epilogue, the pointless Epilogue,

---

* As this book has been prepared Guthrie Moir has begun a series of "Last Programmes" which have replaced the Epilogue format in A-R programmes.

and the Epilogue which is merely a succession of unrelated disconnected talks chosen at random,' said the survey . . . 'great stress is placed upon the value of epilogues being co-ordinated and planned, with possibly the same contributor appearing on successive nights to discuss and pursue a specific subject stage by stage. . . . Coupled with this is a suggestion for religious teaching and doctrine, the fundamentals of Christianity and Bible exposition.' Such programmes have been attempted in the epilogue format, but it is quite clear that while there is a demand for these brief closing programmes in some regions, where other methods have been tried there has been a considerable response.

Whatever may be done about expanding the opportunity in general balance slots in the main programme timing, it seems fairly certain that the Epilogue will be with us for some time to come in commercial television – indeed some companies value it quite highly – and therefore within the limitations imposed by the time of transmission, the low budget and the limited facilities, an imaginative effort must be made to use the time to the best advantage.

In the first section of this chapter we asked what was the relationship between the Christian communicator and the producer in the BBC Religious Department. If we now ask the same question about that relationship in commercial television, we shall find that although in some ways it is similar, in other ways it is quite different. To begin with, what I have said about the need for competence applies equally to both channels. The conception of the effort as a piece of team-work, freedom of expression, and an awareness of the professional skill and integrity of the producers are also common factors. The difference – and again, this is a personal impression, gained from working with a number of commercial companies – seems to me to be evident in two ways. One is the organizational difference. As we have seen, all the producers in commercial television are laymen, and there is no full-time staff of clergy and ministers as there is in the BBC Religious Department. Commercial producers work in close co-operation with their Religious Advisers, who are not full-time television staff.

When a producer is preparing a programme with a commercial company, he is, therefore, likely to be working with a producer whose approach is different from one of the clergy or ministers who would be with him in the BBC. Such a producer is not likely to have been trained formally in theology. This, however, can be seen as an advantage. A producer who is willing to try to seek the insights for which the performer himself is searching, can very often ask questions of the programme which the viewer is likely to ask. Some of the producers I have named, whose religious programmes have been as incisive and penetrating as anything on television, bring to bear on the programme not only their technical ability, but also their experience in other types of programme. This can mean that the programme is helped rather than hindered by the fact that the producer is not a theologian.

On the other hand, of course, it is possible, especially in low-budget programmes, for an inexperienced cleric to be expected to do Epilogues in a small news studio, with few, if any facilities, and with the help of a producer who has no particular interest in the programme beyond his professional concern to put the programme out as painlessly as possible. The time is passing when this was the case, but it is a danger against which all low-budget output has to guard.

When such full-scale productions as 'Sunday Break' or 'About Religion' are treated with care and seriousness, as they are, it is quite obvious that commercial television can produce first-rate religious programmes, and that the difference in approach need not affect the quality of the output, but may have its own distinctive advantages.

The second difference between the two channels is in the type of programme transmitted. This is accounted for in part by the type of audience which is reached. The commercial channel depends upon reaching a consumer-conscious public, who may respond to the advertising which is put out between programmes. Although it is notoriously difficult to make comparative assessments of types of audience, because of the difference in methods of audience measurement techniques, it is evident that the 'mass audience' composed of the bulk of the population is the target of commercial television.[8]

The necessary assumption, therefore, behind every commercial television programme is that it must be on the right level of intelligibility for the audience. This does not mean that ITV audiences are to be regarded as morons – far from it. The rate at which 'serious' programmes have increased in popularity on ITV[9] is evidence that there is a large audience for such programmes, and the demand for clarity and plainness of statement is not to be confused with a need to 'talk down' to the audience. Television is, however, committed to the mass audience, and if profound things are said, they must somehow or other be said with the simplicity which demands very hard work to attain.

If the danger in the BBC's Departmental approach is, as I have suggested, a danger of institutionalism, there is an equal danger that commercial television can become too commercial in its outlook, and covet the mass audience for its own sake.

If the producer of the Christian programme in commercial television is not committed to the Christian point of view, at least he needs to be sympathetic to the Christian attitude, and he must be ready to be fair to the Christian view inherent in the programme. Given those conditions, the religious programme in ITV stands as good a chance of communicating something real about the Gospel as those programmes put out by committed Christians in the BBC Religious Department.

REFERENCES

1 *Hearing, Seeing, Believing* (BBC Publications)
2 Mary Crozier, *Broadcasting*, pp. 177ff.
3 See Appendix I for a summary of programmes and audiences
4 *Religious programmes on Independent Television*, ITA, 1962
5 Redington, ed., *About Religion*, ITA, 1963
6 See Appendix III for details
7 Appendix IV
8 See Appendix V for TAM ratings of ITV Religious Programmes
9 It is claimed that the growth of serious programmes on ITV is very marked. In the London area they have increased from 19 per cent of the programme time in 1956 to 37 per cent in 1963 (*Facts and Figures* January to March 1963, pub. ITA)

CHAPTER 8

WORSHIP ON THE AIR

W E NOW TURN to one aspect of broadcasting which, in my
view, offers special opportunities and presents particular
problems to the Church. It is the broadcasting of worship. This
takes place both on sound and television on Sundays, and during
the week on sound only, in such features as the Daily Service
and Worship for Schools. I am, however, here only concerned
with the present system of broadcasting and televising Church
services on Sunday. This happens in three main ways.

The BBC puts out a Morning Service and a People's Service
each Sunday, and occasional Regional Evening Services. These
are sound programmes.

BBC Television does not put out a service every Sunday, but
does televise public worship on occasions. ITV transmits an act
of public worship every Sunday morning. Details are given in
the previous chapter.

Broadcast worship may, then, be considered in three ways.
Firstly, there is the great State or ceremonial occasion. Such
services as the Coronation, the memorial service for President
Kennedy, and the annual Service of Remembrance at the
Cenotaph, are obvious examples. These are left out of the present
survey. They provide impressive and spectacular moments of
television, but are not representative of the normal worship of
the Church.

Secondly, there is the radio service, and thirdly the service
which is televised. I propose, therefore, to deal with sound radio
briefly before looking at the place and function of worship on
television.

WORSHIP ON SOUND RADIO

As we have seen, public worship is broadcast in two main ways.
The Morning Service type of broadcast is essentially an act

67

of worship in the local Church which is 'overheard' by the microphone, although it will often be specially arranged and may contain unusual features.

In general the BBC seeks in this way to reflect the worshipping life of the Church, reaching many housebound and sick people, as well as those who, for one reason or another, cannot be at Church that day. The service may be regional in the sense that more than one Morning Service is being broadcast at the same time. The audience may be as large as a million people.

Although the preacher who is responsible for the broadcast will be preaching to more people at once than he will in years of his ordinary ministry, he is still required to remember that they are in ones and twos, and therefore his mode of address must not be rhetorical, but personal and direct. Colin James says: 'In choosing Churches we try to find clergy who are prepared to make the necessary adaptation which radio demands of the Ministry of the Word; men who are supported by a live congregation and a tolerably good choir . . . we look for men and Churches ready to serve radio and its audience, and not to exploit it for personal or local prestige . . . to minister to that section of the listening public familiar with the established patterns of worship.'

There can be no doubt that this kind of service has great value, but I wonder whether, in view of the very large output of the BBC on radio, it is not asking too much of the Religious Department to sustain it Sunday by Sunday. In the interests of quality perhaps there is a case for reducing the quantity here, and using the time and facilities which would be saved to better advantage in alternative programmes in which the Christian listener could be helped, though not always in the framework of a traditional act of worship.

For those who find the similar patterns of worship unrelated to their lives, and who are not normally church-goers, the People's Service is broadcast on the BBC Light Programme. This usually runs for four Sundays for each series of services, and is not ordered in the normal patterns of worship. Short addresses, readings and hymns are combined to expound the Gospel to an audience which is not ready to listen to the more formal worship of the Church. This programme reaches perhaps four or five million people, and is popular in more senses than one. There is room in the format of the programme for variation, and an easy, non-technical approach is necessary. Any preacher who has had to do this service will know that it has a salutary effect upon his style. It is not an 'overheard' service in the sense that the Morning Service is, and it requires an imaginative approach which will help the broadcaster to realize that he will be talking mainly to people who are listening while they relax or work in the house on Sunday morning, or who will be hearing the service on a car-radio. This is a service by which many people hear the Gospel who would otherwise not hear it at all, and can be a valuable contribution to the outreach effort of the Church which is involved in the series.

We have already noted the difficulty of broadcasting religious ideas and attitudes without successfully relating the broadcasting to the Christian community. To some extent the radio service can meet this problem.

In my own experience, radio services can be used to reach people personally. To begin with, it is interesting to note that there are larger audiences for radio services than televised services. This may be attributed partly to the fact that more and more people use portable radio sets; the People's Service is part of the mid-morning Sunday output and they pick up the service in the course of their listening.

It is also true, in my own experience, and this is a general reaction, that more correspondence follows a radio service than one which is televised.

There is, then, seemingly a different kind of response to radio services than televised services. I have said that it is possible to reach people personally in this way, and this is done through the correspondence which follows the programme. Not only do many people write to the preacher expressing their opinions – good and bad – of the service. They also often write asking for advice on some spiritual problem, making their own link with the voice they have heard.

It seems that the anonymous voice, preaching, it may be, far away from the home of the listener, is a potential confidant of the kind that is needed. He ceases to be anonymous, of course, once the letter has been written, but he is still probably far enough away to make the approach possible for someone who does not wish to go to his local minister or priest.

F

It is, however, quite possible, as I have found, to put such a correspondent in touch with a sympathetic minister or layman, although I have done so only with the agreement of my correspondent.

In this way the radio service, and the worshipping community, and the individual listener can be linked on occasion. When this happens, there has, surely, been a real communication, and the whole effort has been used for its true purpose.

We need to recognize, however, that this in itself is a limited purpose. There are some things a radio service does not in itself possess. And the principal lack is that of the actual fellowship of the Church itself. It has been emphasized often enough that religious broadcasting cannot 'be' the Church. It can convey something of the Church's character and worship and thought, but it cannot constitute a fellowship of action and response. This inability of both radio and television services to produce a full personal involvement means that we must constantly remember the boundaries which are set by these modes of communication, some of which were discussed in Chapter 5.

If the institutional Church is to use the mass media, there needs to be more thought on the subject of how the effective radio service is followed up, when the contact by correspondence such as I have described is made. Here the Church can really find itself on the frontiers of human need and enquiry, and there is a searching pastoral challenge to make time and give service to those who are quite outside the organized Church, yet turn to it if something in a broadcast service meets their need.

In many ways, when the Church at worship is on the air, it is performing a different function from that which it performs in its usual services.

We may say that when a local Church meets for worship in the usual way, the principal requirement is that the worship should satisfy, inform and inspire those who are in the service. But when the service is being broadcast, the worship itself takes on a new colour, and has a changed objective. More people will be sharing the worship unseen than share it in the Church. It is for 'them' rather than for 'us'. This is a contemporary type of mission to the world.

How the expression of that mission is to be approached can be considered as we now look at the televised service.

WORSHIP ON TELEVISION

There are certain differences between radio and television which it is important to note when we think about broadcasting worship.

The radio listener only hears the spoken word and the music. He can make his own mental pictures, he can concentrate on what is being said, and he can give his undivided attention, if he wishes, to the content of the service.

The viewer who is watching a televised service, however, is not making his own images of the service. The producer is selecting visual images for him. The well-known axiom of the television word – 'The eye always beats the ear' – is particularly applicable here.

In effect the viewer is watching the service through the eyes of someone else – the producer who is selecting the shots which reach the screen. This means that the viewer's involvement is secondhand, that is, he is sharing the worship visually by way of the selectivity of another mind. It also means that he can easily be distracted from the words that are said by the pictures which are being shown.

This visual element is of the greatest importance, for it raises many problems for both the preacher and the producer in the presentation of worship for television.

The preacher will want to present a unified act of worship which is fulfilling the first aim of worship, that of glorifying God, and of creating 'an avenue which leads the creature out from his inveterate self-occupation to a knowledge of God, and ultimately to that union with God which is the beatitude of the soul'.[1] He will want to do this in such a way that the worship performs its function not only for the congregation which is present in Church, but also so that in some way this experience of the meeting with the living God is shared with the viewer.

The producer is confronted with the technical problem of making a series of visual images which will be married to the words which are said, and the movement of the service, so that the whole thing becomes vital for the viewer. He must avoid the risk of becoming what might be called 'shot-hungry'; that is, although he will want to conceive the whole of the service visually, he must not make the words of the service and sermon

meaningless by injecting a feeling of restlessness into the proceedings by forcing picture after picture on the viewer un-
necessarily. On the other hand, if, from the point of view of the
viewer, the service is too static, interest will flag and the preacher's
task will be made more, not less, difficult. The point is illustrated
by the great difficulty which is posed for a man who has to do an
Epilogue, when he is speaking straight at the viewer for as much
as five minutes at a time. This is, perhaps, the hardest thing any
broadcaster is ever asked to do.

Some of these problems are less acute when the service of Holy
Communion is being televised. In this service there is movement
for the camera to follow which is an integral part of the service,
and the visual content of the rite can carry an authority which
stands by itself. This, unfortunately is not true in many Free
Churches. Again, if the Church from which the service is
going out has beautiful architectural features, these can be
used to great advantage in the hands of a skilled and sensitive
producer. Put to good use, the movement of worship, and the
surroundings in which the service is being held can be aids to
the presentation of worship on television, and, at first sight it
would seem that those Churches which have a tradition of
liturgical worship, and buildings of great interest and beauty,
are at a distinct advantage. This, however, seems to me to
depend upon the aim of the service. If it is to be an 'over-
looked and overheard' service, the advantages are clear.
If, however, the aim is to reach people who are not normally
familiar with the worship of the Church, the elaboration of
ritual and even the architecture itself might become the major
focus of interest and the content of the service might be lost.

It is at this point that it might be useful to discuss the presentation of Free Church worship on television. It has been argued
that, because of the plainness of most Free Church architecture,
and the simplicity and fairly static quality of the ordering of the
service, it is much more difficult to make a successful television
transmission of Free Church worship. There may be little for the
camera to 'watch' in movement, and less for it to see in beauty
and shape. This is not a small consideration when it is remembered that during prayers, and congregational hymns, it is
necessary for the picture on the television screen to show something suitable. Endless pictures of the faces of the congregation

are not enough. That these difficulties are real we must admit –
though not all Free Church worship is quite so formless and
dull as may sometimes be suggested!

The very freedom of the ordering of such worship can be
turned to advantage but only if that freedom is used to set
people at liberty to be spontaneous. And this can be done by
creating an act of worship specifically for television. It is true, of
course, that such a programme would not reflect the normal act
of worship at that particular Church. But is it necessary to make
this the only method of televising worship? I think not.

So long as it is made quite clear in the programme announcement what is being done, a communication in terms of worship
can be made about the nature or action of the Church which is
devised especially for television. And this can be a way of presenting the Gospel in terms which at once express the life of the
Church, and the meaning of the Gospel for today, and uses the
medium of television as a vehicle by which this is done, not by
'overlooking' a normal act of worship, but by conceiving that
particular act of worship for that purpose.

An example of such a service is shown in Appendix VI. This
was created in consultation with the producer from the very
beginning. It sought to say something about the function of a
central city Mission by referring to the original intention of those
who began the Methodist Central Hall movement, and tried to
bring the idea up to the present moment by showing within a
framework of worship which followed a definite pattern, the
life and action of the Church in its mission now. Film with
commentary was used, and some of this preceded the service
itself, while some was used during the singing of a hymn. The
sermon was brief and simply summed up what had been expressed in the course of the service by the representative laity
who had spoken and read the Scriptures.

Although the general framework of the service was in the
ethos of the normal worship of the Central Hall in Bristol, the
detailed construction of the service was very different from the
more usual shape of a morning service. At the same time, it
must be said, this did not represent a drastic departure from the
norm, because the morning service in this particular Mission
varies in character, using different forms of service from time
to time.

Thus, the integrity of the programme was secure, because what was being done was not completely alien to the regular members of the morning congregation, and therefore could not be said to be specially set up for television in that sense.

On the other hand, the service was different in the sense that it was prepared with the television transmission in mind, and the congregation was conscious of the fact that it was playing an important part in helping to share something of the work and witness of the Church.

In many ways the Free Churches are, to my mind, ideally placed to experiment in this way, and more could be done to use worship in unusual ways, both in the studio and in the Churches themselves.

If it is objected that this would not reflect the usual life and worship of the Church, perhaps we should consider how little the usual forms of worship really do the work of evangelism, in the sense that worship can be the communication of the Gospel to the man who does not normally hear it. There is a long tradition in the Free Churches that this is at least one important use of public worship. In these ecumenical days, it may be hoped that one of the contributions the non-Anglican Churches could make to the worship and witness of the total Church is the concept of worship as a means of evangelism, as well as a means of grace for the committed. That this is not happening on any large scale in public worship in this country I have already argued at some length in Chapter 1. It is evident that in America also there is concern that the context of public worship is too narrow. Gibson Winter points out that the identification of the forms of the Church with family and residential interest has produced a situation which has led to a restriction of the context of religious life to the most private matters.

'In this sense "public worship" as a common liturgy in which the richness of the Word and Sacrament intersects with the common life of the people has disappeared. We simply do not enjoy the experience of public worship, for the intersecting concerns in the religious contexts do not reflect public matters.

'To this extent the proclamation of the Church occurs in an impoverished context which transmutes the Gospel into a superficial reinforcement of the morality façade overlaying the American pursuit of private matters.'[2]

If, in the twentieth century, public worship is once again to intersect with the common life of the people, television and radio may be one means, and a major means, by which this is done. We cannot, for example, expect to transmit worship which will have a life-changing effect upon those who hear it and see it, unless we are prepared for such a transmission to have an effect upon the Church itself. Any genuine attempt to involve people in the worship of the Church through the mass media, will involve those who are part of the worshipping community in something which will have an effect upon themselves.

At the moment, this is something which many Churches do not wish to accept. They do not mind having 'their' service broadcast, with the small prestige that such an occasion may bring. But many of them do object violently to allowing a broadcast to become a catalyst of change within themselves or their institution.

To face what may happen if the needs of the people who are not in Church are put before the needs of those who are, could be the means of enriching the context in which the Gospel is proclaimed and once again make the worship of Almighty God a powerful and incisive influence in the life of the nation. A television camera will not do that of itself. But a serious attitude to what that camera stands for might purge the worshipping community of its self-absorption and self-interest and make it what it ought to be – a company of believers whose living concern is for those who are without.

REFERENCES

[1] Evelyn Underhill, *Worship*, 1946, p. 18
[2] Gibson Winter, *The Suburban Captivity of the Churches*, 1961, p. 134

CHAPTER 9

THE PREACHER AND THE MASS MEDIA

BEFORE we consider some approaches to writing for television and radio from the preacher's point of view, we must look at the essential problem which he faces. It is a twofold problem. One part of it is the fact that the Gospel is always a stumbling-block to many people, because it is not simply a panacea for all ills, and it cannot be preached or received in the way that a commercial offer is made and accepted.

We are doing something much more profound than offering a spiritual detergent which, if it is used in the right way, will make everything easy and wonderful. The reminder that we are not selling a success-story in any casual fashion, which was Michael Redington's point in his discussion of the programme 'About Religion' (see Chapter 3), is one which we need constantly to bear in mind.

There is a victory in the Christian life, but it is a victory through the Cross. There is life and hope and peace, but it is not the easy and spurious peace of escapism, but the peace which is at the heart of endless agitations.

There is a gift from God, but with the gift goes a demand, the kind of demand which asks that nothing should be held back, and which touches the tenderest spot in us – our selfhood and independence. It is too much for many of us to acknowledge the utter dependence upon the grace of God which is the precursor of all Christian commitment.

Christ brings us forgiveness, but He also reveals the depth of our sin, and the danger we are in. There is nothing in the life or teaching of Christ which can be used to minimize that danger. It is not rhetoric to talk about a man being 'lost' or 'dead' apart from God. When we speak from the standpoint of the Gospel, in the penetrating truth of that Gospel there is much that is unpalatable for modern man.

The Cross, the heart of all true Christian faith, is indeed a stumbling-block, and that is the eternal problem in making the kind of communication of the Gospel which is acceptable to the hearer. We do not seek to preach so that people will accept it, we seek to offer the Gospel so that people can decide for or against it. Paul Tillich made the point at some length, and these words of his are part of his writing which should be in front of every Christian preacher constantly: 'We are asking: how do we make the message heard and seen and then either rejected or accepted? The question cannot be: how do we communicate the Gospel so that others will accept it? For this there is no method.

'To communicate the Gospel means putting it before the people so that they are able to decide for or against it. The Christian Gospel is a matter of decision. It is to be accepted or rejected. All that we who communicate the Gospel can do is to make possible a genuine decision.'[1]

This, then, is the first part of the problem. The fact that in itself the Gospel is open to rejection, and that there is no guarantee inherent in techniques for its acceptance. The realization of that fact would both release a great deal of tension in the mind of the communicator and make his proclamation more incisive.

Nothing is more depressing for a man to concentrate on 'success' in the wrong way, flogging himself mentally and spiritually because the message is not accepted. And this happens to every preacher until he realizes that he is offering decision to his hearer, not acceptance. If there is an awful responsibility on the preacher, in the proper sense of that word, there is also a responsibility upon his hearer.

The preacher's task is to ensure that he discharges his part of the joint responsibility with all the devotion, all the integrity and all the grace that God will give him, and then live and act upon his faith that the Holy Spirit is at work in what he has done. His personal agonizing over the preparation, delivery and content of his message, the costliness of the whole task, is part of his offering of himself to God. But there comes a point when he must recognize that there is nothing more that he can do. The decision is there to be made. And he cannot make that decision for anyone. It is personal. And it is between God and the man who hears and accepts – or rejects.

The second part of the problem which faces the preacher,

however, is his own responsibility, and no one else can take it. It is stated concisely by Tillich in the same chapter of his *Theology and Culture*: 'Christian ministers often, when they feel frustrated, say that Christianity must be a stumbling-block for most people. Nevertheless there are always a few people who come to our Churches for whom it is a stumbling-block. This gives the minister consolation.

'But there are two kinds of stumbling-block. One is genuine. There is always a genuine decision against the Gospel for those to whom it is a stumbling-block. But this decision should not be dependent on the wrong stumbling-block, namely the wrong way of our communication of the Gospel – our inability to communicate. What we have to do is to overcome the wrong stumbling-block in order to bring people face to face with the right stumbling-block and enable them to make the right decision.'[2]

So, fairly and squarely upon the shoulders of the preacher is laid the burden of a right communication. It is at this point that we are obliged to look at the techniques which are required by the mass media.

To begin with, there is a real danger in being so eager to learn the technique that the technique becomes everything and the execution nothing. Anything that I say in this chapter is the result of a working knowledge of preparing scripts for both sound and television programmes, and although I have valued training courses such as I describe in the next chapter, in the end the practical work of getting a script out and then using it is the most useful method of learning. This is a mode of communication in which we learn as we go, and we are never finished with learning. Every programme presents a new problem, and every situation tests afresh the imagination and the ability to 'hear' or 'see' the theme as the listener or viewer will hear or see it.

In any discussion about techniques, then, we must always beware of becoming slaves to the techniques, lest we imagine the technique will bear the weight which should be borne by the content of what is said.

I once knew a minister who had read somewhere that every good preacher kept a card-index file of sermon illustrations. He was determined to be a preacher *par excellence*, and he began to make a file which would be the finest collection of sermon illustrations ever seen. It was a worthy enough endeavour. The only trouble was that his sermon illustration file dominated his life. At one stage it seemed to his friends that he had created a monster he could not control.

Over-emphasis on methods can be a delusion. We can become obsessed with them, so that we are like the centipede in the rhyme who was provoked into wondering, when he walked, which leg came after which:

> *This raised his mind to such a pitch,*
> *He lay, distracted, in the ditch,*
> *Considering how to run.*

We face the old paradox that techniques are necessary, but they must be so part of the man that they are submerged in the final delivery of the truth.

Just as no artist can paint a picture of the human body without knowing something of anatomy and the structure of the human frame, yet his final portrait will be far removed from an anatomical diagram, so the preacher needs to know the techniques and yet be delivered from imprisonment in technique in the last analysis. When the techniques which are required in the mass media are in some respects so different from those already learned by the preacher for his pulpit work, this becomes especially important.

One last word might be said about the preacher who is removed from his familiar surroundings and given the opportunity to communicate his faith in these new ways. It applies to him with more force than to any other broadcaster, and it has to do with the use of techniques.

It is this. Although every gift he has must be brought into the service of the Gospel and every faculty he possesses must be used, he is finally to seek the power of the Holy Spirit as the dynamic of all his work.

It may seem, at first, unnecessary to say that when it ought to be the constant thought of the preacher. Yet one of the perils of preaching is to concentrate on the human side of our preparation, and forget altogether that our central task is not so much to make the communication ourselves, as to help to create those conditions in which God can speak.

The preacher is a servant of God. No technical competence, however expert, can be a substitute for his dependence upon the Holy Spirit as the Revealer of Truth. This is something which must be borne in mind in all discussions about technique. This, however, only underlines the point that he must be a technically competent servant of God.

WRITING FOR RADIO

Whether the script for radio is that of a sermon in a broadcast service, or a talk in some other type of programme, the first thing to remember is that there is a great difference between the written word and the spoken word. Every preacher ought to know this, but it becomes painfully apparent that the difference is not appreciated sufficiently. Someone who is reading a book, or an article, or a sermon, can go over the words again if necessary; there is no chance of a reference back in a broadcast. The word has gone for ever, when it is spoken. This means that the style will be crisp, the sentences will be short, the long parenthesis cannot be used, nor can the rhetoric of the pulpit.

When the preacher is facing a congregation he can assume some things which he cannot safely assume when he faces a microphone. His congregation will be reasonably familiar with the preaching style; with Biblical references (though this is not so true as it once was); and with the kind of religious generalization which is typical of a great deal of preaching. In addition, they have taken the trouble to come to Church, and are therefore predisposed in favour of the sermon they are going to hear.

In broadcasting the preacher is not facing a congregation, he is talking personally to one or perhaps two, at the most three, people. His audience may be rated in millions, but he is addressing them personally. He must not, then, quite obviously, address them like a public meeting.

His preaching style will sound minatory in a broadcast. The declamatory and emphatic attitude he may normally take up in the pulpit will be magnified into a caricature by the microphone and be deeply objectionable to that solitary listener who has to make all the effort in his listening, instead of being met more than half-way by the man at the microphone.

If he uses Biblical references, he will need to explain simply and briefly what they are about, and see that they are made relevant to the life of the man who is listening, and who may never open his Bible, if he has one.

The religious generalization will be shown for what it really is by being exposed to the microphone. It is the kind of thing which has been the 'padding' to many a sermon in Church, and it was caricatured expertly and cruelly in the revue 'Beyond the Fringe', in a sermon which has been recorded, which should be compulsory listening for every radio aspirant.

On the rare occasions when the religious cliché is not being used as an escape from clear thinking, because it has a familiar sound and meaning to the speaker, it is dangerous in a sermon or talk which is being addressed to people who are likely to be completely unfamiliar with the religious mode of address.

It is sometimes said that theological language is a technical language, and that people who are willing to learn a technical language for some hobby such as do-it-yourself radio-receiver building ought to be willing to learn the technical language of religion if they want to understand the Gospel. The weakness of the argument is that religion is supposed to be about life itself, and must be seen to be rooted recognizably in life itself. In any case the Christian communicator needs to make up his mind that people are not going to learn his specialized language, so that unless he can make common cause with them he will be switched off. Even in programmes which may be intended for a specialized audience, the technical language of theology, unexplained and unapplied to real situations, will defeat the aim of the broadcaster. There is no retreat from the necessity of being plain and meaningful to the audience. The point is excellently made by a writer who is discussing writing for engineers. In a book about how to write technical reports, Joseph Racker says:

'The level of writing is established by widely read newspapers, national magazines and books. Similarly, there is an accepted form for writing letters and most people know and recognize this form.

'This is not true of technical writing. A report that is perfectly clear to its writer may be obscure to many readers. Many engineers are unaware of this fact, however. They subconsciously assume that, as in non-technical writing, anything that is clear to them, is clear to others.'[3]

If we substitute 'preachers' for 'engineers' in the foregoing paragraph we have a clear statement about one of the reasons why so many sermons and scripts are obscure.

There is no easy way to achieve the kind of rapport we are talking about. In various books on the subject we can sometimes find sets of rules. Typical of such rules are 'Ten Radio Commandments' for the effective broadcasting of religious programmes, said to have been outlined by 'a famous radio preacher'. They are:

1. Speak in a conversational tone.
2. Take your sermon not from the Bible but from life.
3. Leave out the word 'I'.
4. Neglect the needless.
5. No bunk.
6. No sob-stuff.
7. Make the web of your sermon optimistic, cheerful.
8. Check and recheck your script before delivering . . . for absolute factual accuracy.
9. Keep the word 'not' out of your script.
10. Use no introduction. Plunge right into the middle of the sermon.[4]

It is not likely that a set of rules could be made without it containing some useful hints, but this kind of approach seems too superficial to have any serious effect upon the man who has a deep concern to communicate the Gospel. Of much greater importance is his whole attitude to the job. He will want to look at the idea which is the basis of his script. And looking at it means looking into it, until he has seen everything there is to be seen in it. He will spend more time thinking about what he has decided to say than he will ultimately spend in writing the actual words of the script.

This seems to me to be a very important part of the preparation of the script. It means that the writer must mentally gaze at his idea, much as an artist looks at a scene he wants to paint. That 'seeing' look is of the greatest importance both in the preparation and the actual delivery of the script. There will come a time when the broadcaster will want to be able to take hold of the idea again, so that he is not simply reading the words in his actual broadcast, but re-living the idea he has to communicate. This is the only way of 'getting it off the page' when he delivers the script in transmission.

The business of clarifying and purging the script of non-essentials is the most important part of constructing a script, and the communicator will make his own set of rules as he goes along.

All this is really the attempt to understand the Gospel more deeply all the time – understand it on more than an intellectual level. It is also the attempt to understand the complex world-background against which the Gospel is being delivered.

The Christian is not to be so concerned with 'importing' his Christian idea into the land of secularism, as with finding within the ordinary life of men the springboard from which Christian insights can be applied to the human situation. We do not, in fact, say: 'Here is the truth on my terms, take it or leave it.' We try to say: 'Come with me and we will search for this truth together.'

This will mean a kind of honesty of approach which may bring the preacher face to face with the Gospel for himself all over again. Any man who seeks to confront the living Christ with other people will find himself exposed as well as them. And preachers, no less than other mortals, are reluctant to expose themselves. Sometimes the attempt to get inside the thinking of non-Christians will be a searing experience for the preacher who has normally been accustomed to expounding the Gospel to the faithful few whose expectation is dulled.

It was a non-Christian who said of Jesus Christ: 'He was like some terrible moral huntsman digging mankind out of the snug burrows in which they lived . . . is it any wonder that men were dazzled and blinded and cried out against Him? Even his disciples cried out when he would not spare them the light.'[5]

The beginning of the attempt to confront men with the Gospel is the confrontation of it ourselves. And the measure of our compassion for the difficulty men have in meeting us as we proclaim that Gospel may be the measure of our humility as we hear it ourselves again, as if for the first time.

5. 'Ecumenical Action' (TWW). A discussion between the Bishop of Bristol, the Archbishop of Cardiff, and Monseigneur Joseph Buckley.

6. 'Christmas Story' (TWW). Christine Godwin talks to a young guest.

WRITING FOR TELEVISION

If it is true that lists of rules in themselves cannot provide a ready-made method for the writer of radio scripts, it is certainly true that in preparing television programmes there is really only one rule to remember.

It is that all ideas must be expressed visually. The most damning criticism of a television programme is that it could equally well have gone on sound radio. This criticism could be applied to many religious television presentations.

Perhaps this is partly because the religious programme is sometimes a low-budget production, and, in the case of Epilogues the programme is too short to use film or any kind of visual aids. It may also be due to the fact that a lot of religious programme ideas come from parsons, and most parsons think verbally rather than visually. The tendency to wordiness in religious television may be due to the professional temptation to wordiness which is the parson's special weakness.

The programme may too often be cast in what might be called the 'sermonic' form, and the tendency to question-begging which marks many sermons is carried over into a medium which exposes such an approach mercilessly.

Beyond these considerations, however, is the opportunity which occurs in the type of programme in which such limitations do not apply, and here we meet a difficulty which is not so much the technical problem of writing the actual script, as one of being able to meet the audience in visual terms.

Normally the technical writing of the script can be done by those who are accustomed to handling shot-lists, and setting up the script for the camera – here the producer plays his important part. There is, indeed, a desperate need for professionally-trained script-writers who would produce scripts for religious television, but at present the immediate problem of the Christian communicator is not so much to learn the mechanics of producing a script ready for the studio floor as to explore the possibilities of finding images which will be meaningful to an audience which is not at home with religious images and symbols.

If we work on the assumption that we are trying to communicate to the wide and general television audience, we need to be aware of the fact that when we look for visual images and symbols many, if not all, the traditional Christian symbols have become meaningless in our time.

This much-discussed problem of Christian symbolism is central to our thinking in this field. The symbolic communication which Christians have inherited from their past is inadequate to the task in the new age in which we live, and therefore we have been compelled to re-think the very basis of the means of communication we have to use. This revolution in man's attitude to traditional Christian symbols is of immense importance just at a time when television offers the opportunity it does to use visual symbolism as a means of reaching masses of people with the Gospel. It is no part of the purpose of this book to embark on a detailed examination of the way in which that revolution has taken place, but we must note it carefully, and seek to understand what has happened.[6]

As the Hebrew-Christian tradition grew in the culture of Mediterranean paganism in the first centuries of the Christian Church, it was able to find a means of expression through the patterns of symbolism which had evolved as part of human consciousness from the earliest times. So the development of a dominating group of symbols of a sacramental order became possible – bread and wine, oil and water, and the symbolic meanings which could be invested in the sign of the fish, the Lamb, the Dove, were all used to point the way to the meaning of the supernatural world. The typology upon which these sacramental symbols were based was one already familiar to the world in which the Church worked and witnessed, and so ancient and well recognized ideas were given a new content.

This content continued to be recognized up to the Middle Ages. Indeed the old symbols were canonized by the Church of the Middle Ages so that men were left with no alternative but to use them. It was as though the Church had erected over every other approach a sign which said 'No Entry'. The old symbols were to be discarded only at the peril of man's immortal soul.

The men of the Middle Ages were the last men in history to assume that men may come and men may go, but the great unseen was changeless and eternal, known through the traditional symbols of the former days.

Now came the age of adventure and enlightenment when the

thirteenth and fourteenth centuries produced the beginnings of experimental science, the decline of clerical domination, and the exaltation of reason which was to dissolve the old symbols into superstition, and search for rational and naturalistic accounts of reality. It was the time when 'glass was used not only for church windows depicting the miracles of the Bible and the legends of the saints, but also for lenses in telescopes and micro-scopes'.[7]

This period of the new rationalism was the forerunner of the industrial and scientific revolution in the West which completed the process, and we are thus the heirs of methods of thought about our world which are set within definite limits of space and time. The old symbols of an eternal and 'other' world have been replaced by new ones of status, political power and love, of an order which is of this world.

The evolutionary view of nature has made it increasingly difficult for modern man to see himself as the object of God's care, a creature in God's providence. As Gilbert Cope points out, he sees himself in control, not controlled:

'On the one hand, modern man sees himself as the outcome of an automatic evolutionary process, and on the other hand, he sees himself as being in a position of knowledge and power to control the evolutionary process itself and to substitute human selection for natural selection wherever it may seem to be to his advantage.'[8]

The point was neatly emphasized by two programmes put out in a single week by the BBC in February 1964. One was in Panorama, which dealt with the Indian over-population problem and showed an Indian doctor giving instructions in contraceptive techniques, and the other was one of the series 'Your Life in their Hands', which showed a British specialist helping childless parents to fulfil their longing to have children. Man, not Nature, is here seen to be the controller of the repro-ductive processes themselves.

What meaning the will of God and the providence associated with another world can have to people who see themselves as the arbiters of destiny in this way, is a question to which the Christian communicator must address himself. If the only symbols he has are those of the discarded 'other world' he finds himself rendered inarticulate.

Gilbert Cope's suggestion that we have not achieved a fully integrated world-outlook comparable to that which was built up in antiquity, and which came to completion in the Middle Ages, is used by him to develop his thinking about Church decoration. But as we think about the ancient Creation themes and the new life-directing discoveries of modern man, much of what he says could be applied to the way in which we think about producing visual images for use in television.

'There is a sense,' writes Cope, 'in which we know too much about our environment and ourselves. We certainly know too much about the earth and the solar system and the evolutionary process to be able to make direct use of the symbolism traditionally associated with the theme of Creation. . . . Apparently it was thought perfectly natural at one time to depict a man sticking a pig or treading the grapes as something which ought to be related to his religion; when these carvings were made there was nothing "quaint" about them – they were entirely contemporary and ordinary, so why should we hesitate to have representations of a typist or a panel-beater? Nor need we forget the humour and wit and satire of some of the medieval art. It is a great mistake to confuse seriousness with solemnity.'[9]

It is, of course, a great wrench for any preacher who is steeped in the traditional to recognize that what will seemingly do service for his 'in-group' congregations is completely unacceptable to an 'out-group' mass audience, and it is easy for him to become defensive about the problem. But Gilbert Cope's thoughts about Church decoration contain hints at the way in which modern images of creativity could become a means by which Creation could be seen as an activity which is transcendent. His appeal not to forget wit and satire as tools for the use of the communicator in visual patterns is perhaps likely to evoke a memory of 'That Was The Week That Was'. With its many weaknesses, that controversial programme may have contained a religious motif – David Frost once told me that he wanted to attack 'anything that diminishes men'. There is something here of the truly religious outlook, though not readily recognized as belonging to the institutional forms of religion.

The very violence of the reaction of many religious people to such a programme is indicative of the difficulty which is experienced when the familiar symbolic patterns are deserted, and the new, brash modern symbols are used to try to say something about the meaning of modern life, and perhaps ultimately about the meaning behind it. The failure, even more than the success, of such a programme provides indication of the difficulty. If completely materialistic symbols are the only ones to be used, the materialism and cynicism may be communicated without the transcendent meaning of the symbols getting through to the viewer at all. This happened on a number of occasions in 'That Was The Week' when, for example, for most people Millicent Martin's song about illegitimacy failed to communicate the deep protest within it, and only produced howls of desecration because of the repetition of a certain seven-letter word.

Perhaps this has something to say to us about the dilemma which is produced when all the traditional symbols are abandoned, and only the symbols of the new age are used.

Two alternatives are frequently offered. One is the attempt to communicate the Christian faith by a completely fundamentalist Gospel or a completely authoritative Church. The conservative theological approach is understandable, for at least one of the tasks of the Church is to conserve the truth which it has inherited. But when the conservative says 'I will use no symbols', he is not being fair to himself, for he is very often using symbols which he himself has mistaken for what he calls the literal truth.

The other alternative is that of the positivist who asks the Christian to stop his double-thinking and speak plainly, saying precisely what he means. To this the Christian is bound to reply, 'I can't say precisely what I mean in the way that you ask – and for that matter, neither can you.'

Much of this misunderstanding is based on the delusion that symbols must be taken literally, which, of course, is the one thing that must not happen.

We turn, then, to the new symbols of today. They are not difficult to see, for they are before our eyes in almost every television programme and on every poster board.

F. W. Dillistone has outlined some of them. He says '. . . the dominant symbolism of our own time in the West, and increasing throughout the world, grows out of the assumptions of empirical science. By observation and intelligent action man can secure the satisfaction of life's basic needs. This is not only the case with such obvious requirements as food, drink and shelter, but also with . . . security, freedom, order, significance. And the symbolic expression of those needs is to be found in the constant projection of the image of the one who has achieved success in these areas of experience. The romantic hero, the "star" who succeeds in the struggle with natural circumstances or in the competition with his fellow men, the political leader, the man of recognized genius in any realm of artistic creation – these are the symbolic figures of our time. Lesser mortals gain satisfaction of their needs either by identifying themselves with these symbols of achievement or by attempting to attract some measure of the symbol's "power" into the restricted orbit of their own experience.'[10]

Dillistone points out that the crucial question is whether mankind will go on being satisfied with symbols which represent human life as attaining its maximum in sexual fulfilment, in physical achievement, in political ascendancy, in artistic supremacy. The question might be put another way by asking whether man is going to continue to refuse to look beyond the things of which these are symbols. If so, then we are done for. There is nothing that the Christian can say to a man if those symbols represent the realities for which he lives.

I do not think that he will always be so content, however. And it is the faith that there is more in man than meets the material-ist's eye that is the spur to the search for ways in which to communicate the fullness of the faith to him.

In the meantime, there is no doubt of the efficacy of his modern symbols. However transient they may be, they offer a kind of satisfaction to the man of the world of the 'sixties.

They have their limitations – even the greatest 'star' is mortal, and in any case his hold upon the mass-man is precarious. Even though the 'pop idol' is a precarious man and can be replaced, at least he *can* be replaced with speed and effectiveness, so that there is a continuity in kind, which may be thought to be the new materialistic equivalent of eternal life.

He may fulfil other requirements as a symbol. He is near but not too near the real working life of his devotees. He has the required 'mystique'. He offers hope to imitators. Provided that the sufficient aim is the satisfaction of human needs without reference to the transcendent, he can help individuals to fulfil themselves.

Even where personal fulfilment cannot be direct, there is an indirect satisfaction at feeling that the world, in itself, can be the scene of justice and deliverance. John W. Bachman's observation that the 'Western' television film is Messianic in quality gains point as we see how the myth of the star and the symbol of filmic success can replace all the old ideas. If, in spite of all the evidence of their working world, men can view that world through a rose-coloured zoom lens and be reassured that, after all, the 'goodies' are all in white, and the 'baddies' are all in black, and that there is a mysterious stranger to put all things right, just as the Lone Ranger does, they can find the same sort of comfort, spurious though it may be, as the false comfort which comes from an escapist type of religion.

It is not altogether suprising that when the modern industrial man feels the impact of the scientific revolution, he turns from an emasculated type of religion to his own electronic substitute. To adapt what E. L. Mascall said about the cinema, the sitting-room is his Church, the television set is his altar, the television star is his priest, the television programme is his sacrament, and his idea of heaven is the Television Centre.[11]

In such a situation, a television programme which only presents the traditional symbols must have a very limited use. At best it may inform people about what the symbols are intended to convey to those who recognize them. This would seem to be the equivalent of finding a sermon illustration which needed itself to be interpreted before it could be used to elucidate a point in the sermon. If a symbol has to be rationalized, in fact, it cannot make an effective impact. And most of the traditional symbols of Christianity have to be rationalized to an audience who have no awareness of their meaning.

Can the Christian communicator find any symbol to replace the traditional ones? The clue to an answer to this question may possibly be found in the recognition that there are some symbols which are still potent even in the scientific age.

I would suggest that there are some symbols which are drawn, in the first place, not from the traditional 'religious' field of symbolism, but from mental images of earthly experience.

These are images which were, in the first instance no doubt, used as literal descriptions of the divine world. They are no longer used in that literal sense, yet we cannot discard them, because they are deep in the thought-forms of all men.

They are such symbols as height, time, light and spirit, and each of these offers a starting-point for the visual discussion of reality. There is a universality about them which is admittedly dangerous because if they are merely used as vehicles for generalizations about life, they can be pantheistic in application. Yet this very universality is what commends them as being ways in which reality can be approached.

If they are to be applied as symbols which can link the falsely divided Christian and secular worlds, however, one method of using them is to be avoided. It is the method of dealing with them in a general way for most of the programme, and then at the last moment introducing the Biblical overtones of the theme as an Alice-in-Wonderland type of knockdown argument.

Any application of these symbols to questions about life must spring from within the symbol, and from within life. They may serve as an introduction to the one personal symbol which is recognizable yet rejected – the image of God as He is seen in the living Christ. They are the kind of symbols which can be used to express aspects of the character of the living Christ. And if they can be related to the actual caring Church, which is the body of Christ, the seemingly impersonal symbol of spirit is expressed in the spirit of Christ in men today; and the height of personal aspiration becomes meaningful because men still aspire; and the light of truth is seen to be in men.

Some dramatists have achieved this identification with reality by finding an echo in human consciousness of the truth they struggle to portray. Ibsen and Chekhov have done it. And in some of his plays, Harold Pinter amongst the modern playwrights seems to have the ability to evoke this kind of response. The viewer may begin by looking at the characters in a Pinter play and saying: 'I have never seen anyone like that in my life.' Presently he may say: 'I do know someone like that.' And he may end by saying: 'My God, that's me!'

This is done by statements about the human situation, and these may be no more than descriptions of the situation. The Christian communicator wishes to do more – he wants not only to describe and diagnose, but also to prescribe.

Again, we must ask a question: Is it possible to prescribe in this way, or is it enough to confront men with their situation and help them to a prescription of their own? What will help them to a Christian understanding of their need will not in the end be the image of itself that the Church has managed to project but the reality the image represents.

The Church must be seen to be the very image of Christ in the world, not over against the secular life, but deep in the heart of it, as He was Incarnate, and is in the Holy Spirit today – this is one way of bringing to life the One who is the symbol of all that is pure and true.

Jesus of Nazareth is still, for many people, the epitome of all that is good. Even the Biblical epics of the cinema have not quite managed to overlay the image of strength and goodness that He represents in the minds of the bulk of people. When His life and purpose are portrayed without sentimentality it is possible to find a ground of common agreement and approach. And such symbols as those we have mentioned, basic symbols which need have no immediate 'religious' significance may be brought into service for the purpose. They may be used to show the harmonious order of reality which is seen to be part of our apprehension of the ultimate values of life, yet which transcends human life as we know it.

The Gospel we have to tell is centred in One who is at once firmly placed in history, and who transcends history. The ability to relate that Gospel to the human situation today is essential, but it must not be done so that the transcendent element is lost. It is for this reason that it is suggested that the natural symbols may make a starting point from which the traditional symbols of the faith may be invested with new meaning. In order to do this it is necessary to personalize the natural symbols, and in the great acts of God in Christ they are, in fact, personalized.

The struggle between light and darkness; the depth of degradation and the height of sublime character; the timelessness of the real love of Christ and the passing values of false love of power and pride; the spirit which shows humanity at its most God-like can all be evoked in visual images. An illustration of this can be seen in the script of a programme, 'The Image of Majesty', which was televised on Good Friday 1962 by ATV.[12]

The investment of natural symbols with Christian meaning through the kind of process I have tried to describe is immensely difficult and an even more difficult task is waiting. It is the task of taking the popular symbols of sex, power and achievement, and showing how they may be purified and redeemed so that they are part of a meaning of life which transcends the daily devaluation of them.

These symbols, even in their devalued form, all have to do with essential elements of life, and Christians need to come to grips with them in other than negative ways if they are to be called into service for the One who makes all things new.

The composition of a television programme, then, must first be a visual rather than a verbal composition. It must seek to offer symbols which are recognizable, and not those which have to be rationalized – for, surely, if a symbol has to be rationalized, it ceases to be a symbol. And it must come to terms with the symbols which have reality for the viewer, so that they can become not only the instruments of the redemptive Gospel, but be redeemed themselves from the devaluation they have suffered.

In this task, more important than the task of understanding the mechanics of writing a script,[13] is the need for us to see that the Christian communicator must avoid the trap of making the image he presents more important than the reality he is trying to represent through the image. He is to be concerned to distinguish between the symbol he is using to visualize the fact, and the fact itself.

For the Christian communicator, the beginning is to be made with Himself, not with the people he is addressing, the call of God to him is to understand even the work of writing a script as part of the work of the living Christ in him. This consciousness of the work of the Holy Spirit as Revealer is, for the Christian, the basic acknowledgment of the kind of communication he is to make, and without it all the technique in the world will not help. Some words of A. C. Bridge seem to me to say this quite clearly, in his conclusion to a book which is of great value in thinking about symbolism today:

'The wonder of the Gospel is not that, in New Testament times, there was a sudden crystal outcrop of miracles in the dull limestone of history which, in its passage across time soon reverted to normal again. On the contrary, the real miracle of the Gospel is that God in Christ inaugurated a new age, the characteristic of which is the continuing miracle of life in the

Holy Spirit. Therefore, a renewed understanding of symbolism must lead to the living unity of transcendence and image, which is life in Christ; or it will have failed to have been a Christian understanding. For today, as in New Testament times, men and women are not called primarily to assent to the validity of the images. They are called to *be* the imagery, as the Church is called to be the image of Christ; and no objective study of the New Testament images can lead to a knowledge of their truth unless it lead also to a humble subjective rendering of the self to God as the subject of His artistry, and the work of His hands.'[14]

REFERENCES

[1] Paul Tillich, *Theology of Culture*, 1959, p. 201

[2] Ibid., p. 213

[3] Joseph Racker, *Technical Writing Techniques*, New York 1960, p. 3

[4] Abbot and Rider, *Handbook of Broadcasting*, New York 1957, p. 179

[5] H. G. Wells, *A Short History of the World*

[6] Note the account of this change in F. W. Dillistone, *Christianity and Symbolism*, Collins, 1956

[7] G. Cope, *Symbolism in the Bible and the Church*, SCM Press, 1959, p. 263

[8] Ibid., p. 264

[9] Ibid., pp. 269–70

[10] In an article in *The Christian Broadcaster* April 1963, p. 25

[11] Cp. E. L. Mascall, *Man: his Origin and Destiny*, Dacre Press, 1940

[12] The script and some stills from the programme are published in Redington, *About Religion*, ATV, 1963, pp. 32–41

[13] An example of a script using the symbol of light and attempting to re-invest it with meaning is shown in Appendix VII

[14] A. C. Bridge, *Images of God*, 1960, p. 151

CHAPTER 10

THE CHURCHES AND THE MASS MEDIA

THROUGHOUT this book I have taken the view that the autonomy of the media of radio and television must be respected. The question still remains how television and radio can be called into the service of the Church. Without doubt these media provide an unparalleled opportunity for the proclamation of the Christian faith, if they are taken seriously by the Church.

We may seek to answer the question by making a brief examination of the ways in which the Church at present approaches this task.

We have already seen that, at some levels, there is a fruitful and cordial relationship between the Churches and the broadcasting companies, both BBC and ITV. Through CRAC and the present organization of the Religious Department of the BBC, as well as in the co-operation which is evident in the system of Religious Advisers to the ITA and the various commercial television companies, this relationship can be seen to be of great value (see Chapter 7).

In other ways, also, the interest and concern of the Churches find expression. Each major Christian denomination has its own central committee on Broadcasting and Television, and there is also a Free Church Consultative Committee which, although it has sought no official status, is a useful clearing-house of opinion and judgement and works in a consultative capacity with all the Free Church denominational committees.

In addition to these various bodies which provide a means of oversight on the part of the various Churches, there has been an interesting development in the opening of the Churches Television Training Centre, originally in Tooting and now housed in excellent accommodation in the Methodist Mission House in Marylebone Road, London. It was established in December 1959 under the auspices of the World Council of Christian

Education and it provides training for ministers and laymen in the use of radio and television.

Courses are held throughout the year at the CTTC and in studios which provide, as far as possible, similar conditions to the actual transmission of television and radio programmes. Students on the courses are able to work under instruction. Lectures on various aspects of the mass media are combined with instruction in the use of visual aids for more familiar Church activities. From these courses it is possible to discover men and women with the necessary potentialities for the media, and not the least valuable part of the work of the CTTC is to help ministers and laymen to a more informed appreciation of the significance of television and radio for our times.

Both BBC and ITV have, in various ways, provided courses for ministers and clergy with the co-operation of the Churches. The BBC courses are carried out on a Regional basis, and are generally one-day courses during which participants have an opportunity to do a short closed-circuit television 'appearance'. TWW, the commercial company for Wales and the West, organized a two-day study course which gave junior clergy in the West an opportunity to see something of the company's approach to religious television.

The most ambitious courses in length and approach have been set up by ABC Television, first under the direction of Tom Singleton, and latterly under the direction of Penry Jones. These have been courses lasting four or five days and have included a considerable amount of time for studio work, lectures on many technical aspects, and an opportunity to write and transmit, on closed-circuit television, a thirty-minute programme, as well as instruction on outside broadcasting techniques.

These courses were followed in 1962 by an advanced course, organized by the same company, for a small number of ministers and clergy who had already gained some experience in television. Speaking as one who has had the privilege of being a student on each of the types of training courses I have described, I would say they underline the claimant need for more opportunities for ministers and laity to be trained. I am quite sure that such courses should have more than the limited and somewhat uncertain aim of 'discovering' suitable talent for the media.

That this can happen incidentally is, of course, possible. But by far the most useful function of such courses, especially the shorter ones, is to inform Church spokesmen of the situation in television and radio; sharpen the awareness of such people about the importance of the media, and awaken their informed interest, not only in religious programmes, but in the whole output.

It is certain that the Churches will have to take much more seriously than they have done the need to provide trained men and women who can face the opportunities offered by television and radio. What has been done is excellent in its way, but there must be a more realistic appreciation of the media in the general attitude of the Churches.

If religious television is not merely to survive, but develop, it will have to continue to draw upon the talent which the Church itself possesses. In this situation, the Church plays too passive a role, often being content to wait for television producers to ask for help, instead of being in a position to make active and imaginative contributions through men and women who have been able to appreciate the potentialities of the media.

What I have said about committees and courses may indicate that there are some signs that this is in the minds of Church leaders. But progress is not quick enough, and it may well be that the Church will need to consider whether it should set aside men with experience and potential in far greater numbers than it does at present, so that they can work in depth on the problems and opportunities which these media present. At the moment the self-preoccupation of the Church is seen in a somewhat grudging acknowledgment of the fringe benefits which may accrue in the casual use of television and radio. The Church must not think so much about the advantages it may gain by using the mass media, as about how it can contribute by bringing to bear the Christian insights which it may have or be able to reach.

These insights may also be shared by congregations and members of the Churches who may never get behind the television screen at all. A considerable number of 'Look and Listen' groups are already established. Some are organized through the CTTC, some through such bodies as the National Institute of Education, and the various denominational councils and committees.

Through such groups, Christians can make a very valuable contribution to what the Churches can do. Group-viewing of religious programmes are an obvious activity. But beyond the range of religious television the group can perform a useful function by being a means of constructive criticism and comment about the whole output of television.

Here it is necessary to note that a Christian 'Look and Listen' group has more than a negative part to play. Members of such groups can, of course, keep a watchful eye on the output. But they need to maintain a balanced attitude to the programmes they watch and criticize. Most people would be genuinely surprised if they realized just how much attention is paid to thoughtful and informed comment from responsible viewers. It is all the more vital, therefore, that groups representing the Churches should be prepared to make an effort to understand the nature of the media, and take into account the likely audience for any particular programme which claims their attention.

Merely negative criticism is useless, but any group which really shows that its members are trying to express a serious and in-formed opinion about programmes in a methodical and intelligent way will find ready appreciation coming from the originators of programmes.

Another part of the Churches' role, and one which has not received sufficient attention, is the follow-up to religious programmes. Presumably the Churches wish to reach people with the Gospel through the medium of television and radio, yet all those who are concerned with broadcasting feel that there is a weakness just at the point where the programme ends.

What happens when the microphone goes dead, and the cameras are switched off? There is often a feeling of anti-climax. After all the care in the preparation of the programme, the tension of the actual transmission, the lights go down, the studio empties with magical speed, and the whole thing seems to be over.

Only later, if and when correspondence comes in either to the studio or the broadcaster direct, is there any real evidence (apart from the audience research figures) that anyone has seen or heard the programme.

If there is response, it is haphazardly met, in the sense that the broadcaster himself probably deals with any letters or enquiries as best he can. He may be able to follow through any initial contacts he makes, but pressure of other work is an inhibiting factor in continuing any prolonged effort. Distance from the listener or viewer is another difficulty.

There would seem here to be an aspect of the follow-up which should be the concern of some of the official committees whose job it is to consider the Churches' responsibility.

It might be worth looking into the possibilities of creating an over-all organization which would be available to help those who appear in religious programmes to follow up their contacts in such a way that some kind of concrete response is made by viewers or listeners who have found help in their listening or viewing.

An example of the kind of thing I have in mind is described in an article about Audience Relations in Japan.[1] Admittedly, the situation differs in this country because the Churches, using highly organized methods of follow-up, as shown in this article, are buying time on a commercial basis. With some adjustments, however, the methods they use may have something to say to us here. And certainly their eagerness to make the concern of the Churches a particular concern for the individual rather than a general concern for the mass audience is commendable.

They are also anxious to see that the acceptance of the message of the programme is not merely what they call an abstract acceptance, but a personal one.

Methods of follow-up which are being used are listed as follows:

1. Individual letters.
2. Home visits.
3. Bible correspondence courses.
4. Mail pool giveaways.
5. Introduction letter to the nearest Church.
6. Newspapers (samples sent and subscriptions encouraged); rallies or meetings locally with listeners in Church, hall or home.
7. Pastoral counselling through a 'letter-box' on the broad-cast which elicits feedback and mail response.

H

The most used and most effective means of follow-up is the Bible correspondence course.

The general method is that when the original contact is made, a master card is opened in a central office and a card is sent to the nearest local Church giving the name, address, and any other information.

In each local Church there is a contact-organizer whose job it is to visit or write to the interested listener, help to keep him interested in the course he is receiving by post, help to answer his questions personally, accompany him to Church, and so on.

An example of the effectiveness of the method is that in the Lutheran Hour in Japan, when this localized method of follow-up was used in the Kyushu centre, the statistics showed the following result:

	BEFORE *Local Follow-Up* *percentage*	AFTER *Local Follow-Up* *percentage*
Number continuing second correspondence course	28	54
Number completing course	4	11
Coming to Kagoshima Churches	8·6	17·2

There are many problems to be solved in using such a method, not the least being the problem of how to choose the Church to which the listener should be introduced – an interesting comment on the obstacle to evangelism provided by our divisions. But there must be here an ecumenical venture worth examining.

This may lead us to another feature of the relationship between the Churches and the mass media. It is the effect of television and radio upon the denominational approach of the Churches of this country.

There is a certain protection of interests in the arrangements made in respect of the denominational ratio referred to in Chapter 7, but the particular problem set by the denominational pattern in Britain is one which has been approached with courage by both channels. The first consideration must always be whether the programme is theologically sound and technically competent, and matters of denominational balance must not be allowed to override either of these standards.[2]

The degree of co-operation which has been experienced in television and radio is a challenge to the Church itself. In this field, the paramount aim is to present the Gospel effectively, and denominational interests come second.

This is an expression of the unity Christians can realize in action, and can itself be an important contribution to the ecumenical dialogue. There is a shared sense of commitment, a common realization of the missionary nature of the task, and an excitement which is often lacking in the day-to-day work of the parish or Church institution.

Here, we are not on the defensive, conserving what we can, but on the frontier between faith and unfaith, where risks are to be taken for the sake of the Gospel, and the Christian must learn again to come out from behind his defences into the arena of real debate. All this can have tonic value for the Church which seizes the opportunity. It can also have a salutary effect upon the Church complacent. It renews the vital questions about the function of the Church itself. For example, if a programme is suggested about the actual work of a church in a particular situation, the exposing questions are automatically posed. A commonplace criticism of the Church is that much of its activity is irrelevant, and when this suggestion is made, churchmen frequently go on to the defensive.

But the exposure of the Church to a wide audience demands that the Church should be seen as the effective instrument of the love of her Lord. When the bright light of a 'worldly' medium falls on much of what we accept in the routine of the Church's activity, it may be seen by even a sympathetic viewer as being something less than it ought to be.

The mass media can help in the current re-appraisal of the function of the Church which is so often theoretical, and not often enough practical.

The problem held out by mass communication can be seen by the Christian to be part of the promise of God. Integrity, insight and courage are needed to fulfil the promise. The camera, the microphone, will not do the work for the Christian communicator, but they can be the instruments by which he finds a new and incisive mode of address.

The man with something to say is given an exhilarating and frightening opportunity. He has no armour, save the armour of the truth, and this is an exposition of the deepest level of his character and belief. In some ways this may be a pitiless revelation of the poverty of man, but if in that poverty the riches of Christ are seen, then all is accomplished, and the Christian communicator's work is begun.

At the last, he must be able to say:

'It was there from the beginning; we have heard it; we have seen it with our own eyes; we looked upon it and felt it with our own hands; and it is of this we tell. Our theme is the word of life.'[3]

REFERENCES

[1] In *The Christian Broadcaster*, October 1963, p. 13
[2] See *Religious Programmes on Television*, ITA, 1962, p. 25
[3] 1 John 1. 1, 2

APPENDIX I

shown as percentages of the population of the United Kingdom aged
5 and over

100 per cent = approximately 49,000,000

HOME SERVICE		per cent
Monday–Friday		
6.50 a.m.	Lift Up Your Hearts	1·3
7.50 a.m.	,, ,, ,, ,,	4·7
10.15 a.m.	The Daily Service	0·5
(*For comparison:*	7.00 a.m. News	5·7
	8.00 a.m. News	11·5)
Sunday		
7.50 a.m.	The First Day of the Week	0·3
9.45 a.m.	Morning Service	1·8*
7.45 p.m.	{ The Way of Life (on some regions)	0·3
	{ Religious Service (on other regions)	0·3*
(*For comparison:* Sunday,	8.00 a.m. News	2·1
	10.00 p.m. News	0·9)

LIGHT PROGRAMME		
Monday–Friday		
9.55 a.m.	Five to Ten	8·8
(*For comparison:* 9.00 a.m. Housewives Choice		17·6)
Sunday		
11.30 a.m.	People's Service	11·3
8.30 p.m.	Sunday Half Hour	2·7
(*For comparison:*	10.30 a.m. Easy Beat	18·5
Sunday,	7.30 p.m. News	1·9)

* Combined audience for different Religious Services in various regions.

BBC-TV

Wednesday

11.15 p.m. app.	Viewpoint	0·8
11.30 p.m. app.	Late Night Final	0·6
(*For comparison:* 11.00 p.m. app. News Extra (Wed.)		2·6)

Sunday

10.30 a.m.	Morning Service	0·5*
11.00 a.m.	Seeing and Believing	0·1
6.15 p.m.	Meeting Point (including audiences for Scottish Meeting Point)	6·4
6.45 p.m.	Sunday Story	4·5
6.55 p.m.	Songs of Praise	9·6
10.45 p.m.	Meeting Point (repeat)	1·1
(*For comparison:* Sunday, 11.30 a.m. Keeping Fit		0·7
	Sunday, 6.10 p.m. News	13·1
	Sunday, 10.00 p.m. News	10·5)

ITV

Sunday

6.15 p.m.	The Sunday Break	6·0
7.00 p.m.	About Religion	5·0
(*For comparison:* Sunday, 6.05 p.m. News		10·0
	Sunday, 7.25 p.m. News	7·0

There is usually a Sunday Morning Service at 11.00 a.m. but, as audiences for ITV are given to the nearest whole number, the audience is nearly always '–' (i.e. less than 0·5 per cent), only once in the fourth quarter was 1 per cent registered, though ITV's transmission of the Service of Remembrance had an audience of 3 per cent. There are other Religious broadcasts on ITV at various times but, as these are not usually carried by all transmitters at the same time, it is very difficult to sort them out.

(These statistics were supplied by the Audience Research Department of the BBC.)

---

* This average does not include the audience for the Service of Remembrance (11·9 per cent) or for the President Kennedy Memorial Service from Westminster Abbey (2 per cent).

APPENDIX II

ITV Religious Output

Programme	Description	Company	Mins.	Time and Day	Area
About Religion	Discussion, Drama	ATV	25	7.0 Sun. 3 wks in 4	N
A Box of Birds	Children's prog.	ATV	30	12.15 Sun. to June	P
Church in View	Discussion	CHANNEL	30	10.30 Mon. (mthly)	L
Church Service	Morning service	ATV/ABC	75	11.0 a.m. Sun. (wkly)	P
		ANGLIA			
		TYNE TEES/			
		SOUTHERN		(occasionally)	
Contact	Parables in modern living	BORDER	5	6.55 Sun. (mthly)	L
The Day is Ended	Epilogue	CHANNEL	5	Close. Wed., Sun.	L
End the Day	Epilogue	ULSTER	5	Close, Daily	L
Epilogue	Epilogue	ANGLIA	5	Close, Mon.-Sat.	L
Epilogue	Epilogue	TYNE TEES	5	Close, Daily	L
Epilogue	Epilogue	A-R	5	Close, Mon.-Fri.	L
Epilogue	Epilogue	ATV	5	Close, All week	L
Epilogue	Epilogue	ABC	5	Close, Sat., Sun.	L
Evening Prayers	Epilogue	GRAMPIAN	5	Late, Daily	L
Evening Worship	Studio service	GRAMPIAN	25	7.0 Sun. (alt)	L
Everyman v. Christ	Holy Week series	TWW	10	Late Mon.-Sat., April	P
Faith For Life	Epilogue	WESTWARD	5	Close, Daily	L

Food For Thought	Documentary	ANGLIA	25	7.0 Sun. (occasional)	L
The Good News	The Bible in story and song	SCOTTISH	20	2.25 Sun., Sept.	L
In Our Time	Religious talk	ANGLIA	5	6.55 Sun. (mthly)	L
Late Call	Epilogue	SCOTTISH	5	Close, All week	L
Let's Face Facts	Discussion	TWW	20	2.05 Sun., 11.40 Fri. (repeat) July-Oct.	L
Life Begins on Sunday	Religious magazine	SCOTTISH	25	2.20 Sun., Oct.	L
A Living Way	Discussion	GRAMPIAN	30	10.45/11.15 Thu., July-Sept.	L
The Living Word	Epilogue	SOUTHERN	5	Close, Daily from May	L
Living Your Life	Discussion, report	ABC	25	7.0 Sun. 1 week in 4	N
One Man's Road	Epilogue	SOUTHERN	5	Close, Daily, Apr.-May	L
Postscript	Epilogue	ANGLIA	5	Close, Sun.	L
Seek the Truth	Discussion	SCOTTISH	30	3.15 Sun. to July	L
Seven Deadly Sins	Discussion	TWW	20	1.48 Sun., 11.40 Fri. (repeat) from Nov.	P
The Summing Up	Epilogue	TWW	5	Close, Sun., Fri.	L
Sunday Break	Magazine for young people	ABC	45	6.15 Sun. 3 wks in 4	N
Thought For The Day	Prologue	ATV	2	12.45 Mon.-Fri.	L
The Twelve Articles	Discussion	TWW	20	2.0 Sun., 11.40 Fri. (repeat) Apr.-June	L
Watch and Worship	Studio service	ULSTER	25	7.0 Sun. (mthly)	L

L. Local. P. Part Network. N. Network. Unless otherwise stated, the lists refer to 1963 and p.m.

N.B.: L = London, M = Midlands, N = North, CS = Central Scotland, W = Wales, S = South, NE = North

East, EA = East Anglia, U = Ulster, SW = Westward, B = Border, NS = Grampian, NW = Wales West & North.

The figures above do not include Channel Television.

		Tamrating	Taken mainly by:
Sunday Church Service	11.00 a.m.	2	All exc. CS, U, NS & NW
10 Nov. Service of Remembrance	10.45 a.m.	8	All exc. NW
24 Dec. Carol Service	4.15 p.m.	8	All exc. M, N, CS, W & NS
24 Dec. Watchnight Service	11.48 p.m.	10	Taken by CS, NS
24 Dec. Sung Eucharist	11.57 p.m.	9	All exc. CS, B & NS
25 Dec. Church Service	11.05 a.m.	5	All exc. CS
25 Dec. Nativity	12.10 p.m.	3	All exc. N, CS, W
25 Dec. Christmas Message	6.20 p.m.	18	All exc. N, CS, NE, EA, B & NS
Sunday Break Sunday	6.18 p.m.	22	All
22 Dec. Festival of Carols	6.16 p.m.	27	Taken by CS, S, U, & B
1 Dec. Memorial Service	6.18 p.m.	23	All
About Religion or ⎫ Living Your Life ⎬ Sunday	7.00 p.m.	21	All
	7.00 p.m.	19	
10 Nov. We Shall Remember Them	7.00 p.m.	29	Taken by CS, U & B
24 Nov. Requiem Statesman	7.00 p.m.	00	All exc. NW
29 Dec. No Star on the Way Back	7.00 p.m.	19	All
Film Premiere Sunday	4.30 p.m.	37	L, SW, NW
Film Premiere or The Big Film Sunday	4.37 p.m.	43	M, N & S
The Greatest Show on Earth Sunday	7.28 p.m.	40	M, N, W, EA, SW, U, NS, NW & sometimes S & B
The Saint Sunday	7.28 p.m.	47	L, NE and sometimes S & B
10 Nov. Royal Variety Command Performance	7.29 p.m.	81	All

APPENDIX III

Everyman v. Christ

Holy Week 1963 – *Television Wales and the West.*

Ratings compared with preceding and succeeding programmes.

Monday

Time	11.07 p.m.	11.40 p.m.	11.50 p.m.
Title	The Cheaters	Everyman v. Christ	Tempo
Rating	19	7	3

Tuesday

Time	11.07 p.m.	11.30 p.m.	11.40 p.m.
Title	Test Pilot	Everyman v. Christ	World in Action
Rating	28	10	5

Wednesday

Time	10.05 p.m.	10.40 p.m.	10.56 p.m.
Title	Tahiti (Documentary)	Everyman v. Christ	The Plane Makers
Rating	24	18	20

Thursday

Time	11.00 p.m.	11.25 p.m.	Close Down
Title	Interpol	Everyman v. Christ	
Rating	30	16	

Friday

Time	10.15 p.m.	10.45 p.m.	10.55 p.m.
Title	In the News	Everyman v. Christ	Laudes Evangeli
Rating	36	24	6

Saturday

Time	11.05 p.m.	11.26 p.m.	11.36 p.m.
Title	On The Braden Beat	Everyman v. Christ	Adventures of Seahawk
Rating	21	20	19

From Monday to Friday it was observed that the graph line of the TAM rating chart remained constant from the time Everyman v. Christ began to the time it finished.

APPENDIX IV

Times of Going to Bed Among Adults in ITV Households and all Households (London Area)

(Summarized from a survey prepared by Nowland and Co. Ltd., for Associated-Rediffusion Ltd., June 1963.)

ITV HOUSEHOLDS

The basic sample was of 2,115 adults. The following figures were significant for the purpose of considering potential viewers of the late night epilogues:

17 per cent went to bed before 10.29 p.m.
17 per cent went to bed between 10.30 and 10.59 p.m.
66 per cent went to bed at 11 p.m. or later.

ADULTS LIVING IN ALL HOUSEHOLDS

The basic sample here was 2,548 and comparable figures were as follows:

18 per cent went to bed before 10.29 p.m.
16 per cent went to bed between 10.30 and 10.59 p.m.
66 per cent went to bed at 11 p.m. or later.

The breakdown of age groups of adults living in ITV households was of special interest.

In age group 25-34: 73 per cent went to bed after 11 p.m.
In age group 35-44: 70 per cent went to bed after 11 p.m.
In age group 45-64: 66 per cent went to bed after 11 p.m.

APPENDIX V

NUMBER OF HOMES ('000's) – DECEMBER 1963

Area	TV Homes	ITV Homes	Total
London	3,848	3,292	4,640
Midlands	2,249	1,936	2,617
North	3,796	3,407	4,500
Scotland	1,081	967	1,319
Wales & the West	1,047	843	1,428
South	1,114	886	1,407
N. East	728	669	883
E. Anglia	589	479	761
Westward	426	320	513
Ulster	234	214	374
Border	142	118	169
Grampian	239	165	288
Total exc. overlap	14,235	12,960	17,158

TAMRATINGS AVERAGED OVER 4th QUARTER 1963
1. Epilogues – W/E 17th November 1963

	Tamrating
London	4
Midlands	11
North	3
Scotland	6
Wales	13
South	3
N. East	8
E. Anglia	4
Westward	2
Ulster	12
Grampian	1
National Average	6

APPENDIX VI

Morning Service

from the Methodist Central Hall, Bristol
Superintendent Minister: the Rev. Leslie J. M. Timmins.
Singing led by the St Mary Redcliffe School Choir (conductor: Peter Fowler).
Organist: John Gillett.
Producer: Kenneth Savidge.
TRANSMISSION: Sunday, 16 June 1963.

My name is Leslie Timmins and Bristol Central Hall is where I'm the Superintendent Minister. This Hall was opened by the President of the Conference in 1924 – it was called 'the home of the people; the Church of the workers and the House of God'. The idea of these Methodist Central Halls – you'll find them in most of our big cities – grew up towards the end of the last century.

It was essentially an evangelistic idea which recognized that there were large numbers of people in industrial England who were completely separated from the life of the Churches.

The Central Hall was to provide a place of worship and preaching and a headquarters for evangelism, fellowship and service. When this Central Hall in Bristol was opened on a rainy April afternoon about forty years ago, it was during a period of slump and depression, and the Hall was surrounded by a dense population living in poverty.

Boys and girls were gathered in off the crowded streets. Soup and dinners were provided for workless men and their families.

Marching miners, on their way from South Wales to London, were given board and lodging at the Central Hall.

But that was nearly forty years ago, and great changes have taken place. The blitz destroyed a great deal of the centre of Bristol.

Sound
The densely packed population was being re-housed on new estates, and we've become what it is fashionable to call a 'down-town church'.

What then is the purpose of a central city Church like this in the 1960s? When we meet here are we anything more than a small gathering of the faithful nostalgically remembering the past?

113

Well that's a very good question and to answer myself, obviously I
hope the answer is no – because I believe there's one job a place like
this can do. Not only have people moved away from us physically
but they've also moved away from us spiritually. How are these
people to be reached by the Christian Gospel? And even suppose they
recognize a need that they feel might be met for them by the Christian
Faith, how do they find contact with the Church?

For many people, to go into a local Church where everybody knows
them after an absence of years, can be an embarrassing experience
and one that they are not too ready to try. But in a Church in the
centre of a city where they can at least, at first, be lost anonymously
in a large congregation, without the immediate need of identification,
there can be a gateway into the life of the Church and the Faith it
proclaims. It is for this reason that I believe there is a greater need
than ever for the Central Hall in these days.

There is an expanding opportunity for the Church to use places
like this in its outreach, and this morning we invite you to join in a
service which we hope will show you that at the heart of this kind
of mission, there must be a believing, worshipping and praying
community.

Introit:

> Break forth, O beauteous heavenly light,
> And usher in the morning,
> Ye shepherds shrink not with afright
> But hear the angel's warning,
> This child now weak in infancy,
> Our confidence and joy shall be
> The power of Satan breaking,
> Our peace eternal making.

Invocation: (Minister)

Eternal God, our Maker and our Lord, Giver of all grace, from
whom every good prayer cometh, and who pourest out upon all who
seek Thee the spirit of grace and supplication: deliver us when we
draw nigh to Thee from all coldness of heart and wandering mind;
fill us with holy, peaceful and gracious thoughts; that with steadfast
mind and kindled affections we may worship Thee in spirit and in
truth; through Jesus Christ our Lord. Amen.

Congregation

Our Father which art in heaven, Hallowed be Thy Name, Thy
kingdom come. Thy will be done. Give us this day our daily bread.

And forgive us our trespasses, As we forgive them that trespass against us. And lead us not into temptation; But deliver us from evil. For thine is the kingdom, the power and the glory, for ever and ever. Amen.

Minister announces hymn. Organ Plays Over Tune

> Lord of all being, throned afar,
> Thy glory flames from sun and star;
> Centre and soul of every sphere,
> Yet to each loving heart now hear.
>
> Sun of our life, Thy quickening ray
> Sheds on our path the glow of day;
> Star of our hope, Thy softened light
> Cheers the long watches of the night.
>
> Our midnight is Thy smile withdrawn,
> Our noontide is Thy gracious dawn,
> Our rainbow arch, Thy mercy's sign;
> All, save the clouds of sin, are Thine.
>
> Lord of all life, below, above,
> Whose light is truth, whose warmth is love,
> Before Thy ever-blazing throne
> We ask no lustre of our own.
>
> Grant us Thy truth to make us free,
> And kindling hearts that burn for Thee,
> Till all Thy living altars claim
> One holy light, one heavenly flame.

Minister

Our worship this morning has been designed to offer to God the work of Christian Education in this Church. The Service is divided into six short sections, each following the same pattern, and each including a reading from the New Testament, and we shall be dealing with the various aspects of Christian Education from childhood to adulthood, and as today is our Sunday School Anniversary, we begin appropriately with the Sunday School.

John Payne

I was brought to Church when I was a baby to be baptized. As I grew up the Sunday School kept in touch with my parents until I was old enough to come to Sunday School. Here I learn the stories of Jesus – how He went about doing good and how I can learn to live like Him.

We try, like Jesus, to help other people as you'll see in a moment. From time to time we take presents to some old people who are our neighbours down the street, as you'll see in a moment.

Minister

Let us offer to God the work in this Church for children, as we sing the hymn 'My Faith it is an oaken staff'.

Organ Plays Over Tune

My Faith, it is an oaken staff,
The traveller's well-loved aid,
My Faith, it is a weapon stout,
The soldier's trusty blade.
I'll travel on and still be stirred
By silent thought or social word;
In toils a pilgrim undeterred,
A soldier unafraid.

I have a captain, and the heart
Of every private man
Has drunk in valour from His eyes
Since first the war began.
He is most merciful in fight,
And of His scars a single sight
The embers of our failing might
Into a flame can fan.

I have a Guide, and in His steps
When travellers have trod,
Whether beneath was flinty rock
Or yielding grassy sod,
They cared not, but with force unspent,
Unmoved by pain, they onward went;
Unstayed by pleasures, still they bent
Their zealous course to God.

My Faith it is an oaken staff;
O let me on it lean.
My Faith, it is a trusty sword;
May falsehood find it keen.

Thy Spirit, Lord, to me impart,
O make me what Thou ever art –
Of patient and courageous heart,
As all true saints have been.

Lesson – (Rex Oram) Mark 10 v. 13–16
They brought children for him to touch; and the disciples scolded them for it. But when Jesus saw this he was indignant, and said to them: 'Let the children come to me; do not try to stop them, for the Kingdom of God belongs to such as these. I tell you whoever does not accept the Kingdom of God like a child, will never enter it.' And he put his arms round them, laid his hands upon them and blessed them.

Minister
When John Wesley began to preach all over England in the eighteenth century, he found that the people who responded to his message needed fellowship and the chance to grow in the knowledge of their new-found Faith. He formed Class meetings – small groups of people who deepened their Faith in thought and action. Today we apply the same principle here in Bristol. From Sunday School young people go on to join a group which meets on Sunday afternoons and then joins in the worship on a Sunday evening.

Hilary Knowles
I am seventeen. Each Sunday I meet with other young people like myself to think about the Christian Faith and how it applies to daily living. Like the children in the Sunday School we try to do more than talk. For instance, we've just recently reached the first hundred pounds towards the cost of a tractor for an under-privileged community.

Minister
Let us offer to God all that we learn and all that we do for others. O God, we pray Thee to use our service – not our patronage, or our desire for power, or our pleasure in meddling in other people's affairs, but our friendship – to build a better world. Help us to put co-operation where there is rivalry, unselfishness where there is selfishness, courage where there is despair, energy where there is listlessness. So may we work, with all who want Thy kingdom to come, for the conquest of disease, the building of noble and spacious towns, the abolition of poverty, and above all that all men and women may come from fear and the slavery of self-indulgence into the freedom of the children of God. Through Jesus Christ our Lord. Amen.

I

Lesson – Peter Lawman Matthew 25 v. 34–40

Then the King will say to those on his right hand: 'You have my Father's blessing, come, enter and possess the kingdom that has been made ready for you since the world was made. For when I was hungry you gave me food; when I was a stranger you took me into your home, when naked you clothed me; when I was ill you came to my help, when in prison you visited me.' Then the righteous will reply, 'Lord, when was it that we saw you hungry and fed you, or thirsty and gave you drink, a stranger and took you home, or naked and clothed you? When did we see you ill or in prison, and come to visit you?' And the King will answer, 'I tell you this, anything you did for one of my brothers here, however humble, you did for me.'

Alice Pope

Christian Education does not stop at seventeen. In wives' groups, women's meetings, and the work of women generally we try to face the issues of Christian standards in family life, and through women's work we provide money for the missionary work of the Church overseas.

For instance, our Bible Class on a Sunday afternoon supports a Bible Woman in India, and has done so for many years.

Minister

Let us offer to God the work of the World Church as we sing our next hymn:

Organ Plays Over Tune

> None other Lamb, none other Name,
> None other hope in heaven or earth or sea,
> None other hiding-place from guilt and shame,
> None beside Thee.

> My faith burns low, my hope burns low;
> Only my heart's desire cries out in me,
> By the deep thunder of its want and woe,
> Cries out to Thee.

> Lord, Thou art life, though I be dead;
> Love's fire Thou art, however cold I be:
> Nor heaven have I, nor place to lay my head,
> Nor home, but Thee.

Lesson – Sister Yvonne Hunkin Matthew 28 v. 16–20

The eleven disciples made their way to Galilee, to the mountain where Jesus had told them to meet Him. When they saw Him, they fell prostrate before him, though some were doubtful. Jesus then came up and spoke to them.

He said: 'Full authority in heaven and on earth has been committed to me. Go forth therefore and make all nations my disciples; baptize men everywhere in the name of the Father, and the Son and the Holy Spirit, and teach them to observe all that I have commanded you. And be assured, I am with you always, to the end of time.'

Sydney Pillinger

Today, new ideas are constantly challenging the Christian Faith. We must always be ready to talk with and meet people's objections to it. To help us do this we extend the work of the Christian Education through a group we call 'Meeting Point'. It is intended to be a place where members of this congregation can learn together as they mature in Christian experience. Through this group we are trying to learn how we can extend the outreach of this Mission in the city; how we can care for people and help them to be part of the Christian community.

Minister

Let us offer this work as we sing our next hymn:

Organ Plays Over Tune

Forth, in thy Name, O Lord, I go,
My daily labour to pursue,
Thee, only Thee, resolved to know
In all I think, or speak, or do.

The task Thy wisdom hath assigned
O let me cheerfully fulfil,
In all my works Thy presence find,
And prove Thy acceptable will.

Thee may I set at my right hand
Whose eyes my inmost substance see,
And labour on at Thy command,
And offer all my works to Thee.

Give me to bear Thy easy yoke,
And every moment watch and pray,

And still to things eternal look,
And hasten to Thy glorious day:

For Thee delightfully employ
Whate'er Thy bounteous grace hath given,
And run my course with even joy,
And closely walk with Thee to heaven.

Lesson – Jack Spiller Ephesians 3 v. 14–19

With this in mind then, I kneel in prayer to the Father, from whom every family in heaven and on earth takes its name, that out of the treasures of his glory he may grant you strength and power through his Spirit in your inner being, that through faith in Christ may dwell in your hearts in love. With deep roots and firm foundations, may you be strong to grasp with all God's people what is the breadth and length and height and depth of the love of Christ and to know it, though it is beyond knowledge. So may you attain to fullness of being, the fullness of God himself.

Ray Giffard

I am a student from Didsbury Theological College – the oldest Methodist Theological College which transferred to Bristol from Manchester at the end of the Second World War. Each week some students spend time in visiting and taking part in the life and work of this Mission. We learn, in this practical way, to be more fully equipped to do our work when we leave college – to do the jobs we believe we are called to do.

Minister

O God, our Father, help us to prepare ourselves faithfully for the tasks of the new age. Give us an overmastering desire for truth which will free us from the slavery of prejudice and lazy thinking. Give us the courage to think freely and to maintain the truth in the teeth of public opinion. Make us ready for responsibility, and if it comes to us now or later, help us neither to refuse it because of our unworthiness nor to be corrupted by it in our souls. So help us to meet the hour in which we live as the loyal followers of Jesus Christ. This we ask for His Name's sake. Amen.

Lesson – Ray Giffard Colossians 1 v. 15–20

He is the image of the invisible God, his is the primacy over all created things. In him everything in heaven and on earth was created, not only things visible but also invisible orders of thrones, sovereignties, authorities, and powers; the whole universe has been created through him and for him. And he exists before everything, and all things are held together in him. He is, moreover, the head of the body, the church. He is its origin, the first to return from the dead, to be in all things alone supreme. For in him the complete being of God, by God's own choice, came to dwell. Through him God chose to reconcile the whole universe to himself, making peace through the shedding of his blood upon the cross – to reconcile all things, whether on earth or in heaven, through him alone.

Minister

We have seen that Christian Education is not to be confined within the walls of the Church. In the community as well as in the schools, the work goes on. Here at the Central Hall, we work closely with our friends in the Anglican church at St Mary Redcliffe – and in our work we are aiming to show our unity in the Gospel.

The Redcliffe School Choir has been leading our singing this morning, and as we offer to God the work of Christian Education in the schools, of this city, they sing the anthem 'O come ye servants of the Lord'.

Anthem

O come, ye servants of the Lord,
And praise His holy Name,
From early morn to setting sun
His right on earth proclaim.
                    (whole verse again)

His laws are just, and glad the heart
He makes His mercies known;
Ye princes come, ye people too,
And bow before His throne.
                    (whole verse again)

Address: Colossians 1 v. 10

We ask God that you may receive all wisdom and spiritual understanding for full insight into His will, so that your manner of life may be worthy of the Lord and entirely pleasing to Him. We pray that you may bear fruit in active goodness of every kind, and grow in the knowledge of God.

The theme of this service has been Christian Education for life. We have been trying to say, in one way and another, that the Church is a place for learning how to live. And that is something we all have to do, whether we like it or not.

From the moment we are born we all start on this business of learning what life is about, and how to make the best of it.

Of course for most of us life is not one long series of crises, but we all have decisions to make, and moments when we know that what we decide is going to make a lot of difference to us. Whether it's the 11+ exam, or a new job, whether it's the moment we meet the girl or boy we want to marry, or perhaps the day when we first hold a child of our own in our arms, life is always presenting us with occasions when we feel the need of guidance and help—when we know the need to be equipped to do the right thing.

And one of the discoveries we can begin to make in the Christian Faith is how to become the kind of people who are ready for what life brings. In this prayer of Paul's, you'll notice, he asks that we might be given spiritual understanding, (insight into the will of God), and the ability to be active in goodness, and grow in the knowledge of God. It's not an accident, of course, that he has put *together* both theory and practice, in this prayer.

Paul asks that spiritual understanding and the knowledge of God may go together with the steady and sometimes hard obedience to the will of God which makes sense of life. And sometimes it can be hard.

It is a complete misunderstanding of religion to regard it as an escape from life. When we came into this Church this morning for worship, we weren't running away from life, trying to shut the Church doors and hide from reality. We were trying to face life, at its best as well as at its worst, find out what it means, and ask for strength and courage to live it well.

The God we know in Jesus Christ does not promise us any short-cuts to success. Instead He shows us the road which makes sense of all the factors in this mysterious world, and offers us His presence and His strength so that we can make the journey in the right direction. When we learn to say this prayer of St Paul's for spiritual understanding, we are, in fact, on the right road – we are learning to use our religion not to escape from life, but to use it as we ought to – the light by which we can see what is worthwhile, and the power by which we truly live.

So, in the first place, we have been offering our lives to God in worship, so that we can understand that those lives of ours have meaning because they are part of God's purpose in the world.

But the attempt to understand life from God's point of view also means something for other people as well as ourselves. We learn, in fact, that you can't keep yourself to yourself.

Spiritual understanding means that we will learn to have a sympathetic response to the needs of other people. When we learn to distinguish between what is good and bad, true and false, we also learn to be sympathetic to other people because we recognize in their difficulties, the kind of trouble we've had with ourselves. We learn, in fact, to help each other, and not to condemn. And we learn what a lot of goodness there is in people and in the world.

Of course there's plenty to condemn in this crazy society of the 1960s. It was recently stated that for every £1 spent on gambling in this country, only $4\frac{1}{2}$d. is spent on scientific research. We are a mixed-up lot when we get our priorities muddled like that. But we won't solve that kind of problem by condemning the gamblers. We've got to try to understand the pressures which are so great that people can't learn to use the tremendous resources of the modern world constructively.

That, of course, is the way of Jesus Christ. No one was so good as He was. No one spoke so plainly about good and bad in people. But no one was so understanding. He never suggested that goodness didn't matter, but in Him that goodness reached out to everyone, to understand, to lift up, and to forgive.

And this is the gift we seek, if our lives make sense – the gift of understanding, the ability to discern what is true and what is false, and the readiness to reach out in love and understanding to others. You will have noticed in this service how many different people have taken part in it. That's because we see this as a picture of what the Church is meant to be – not the building – not the organization. They have their place, but they are not the Church. Not the Minister on his own. Not the people by themselves. But Minister and people. Both. And both together. The family of God concerned about the whole family of mankind. So that together we might search for what we have called spiritual understanding of life. So that we might learn to live together, and together with God, in the World He has given us, and find out what life is really like and live it well.

This is Christian Education for life. And it begins with the beginners in the Sunday School, and it goes on through the seven ages of man. And it never stops, because we know that we are learners all the time. For that's what the word 'disciple' means.

Minister announces hymn. Organ Plays Over Tune

> Fill Thou my life, O Lord my God,
> In every part with praise,
> That my whole being may proclaim
> Thy being and Thy ways.

Not for the lip of praise alone,
Nor e'en the praising heart,
I ask, but for a life made up
Of praise in every part:

Praise in the common things of life,
Its goings out and in;
Praise in each duty and each deed,
However small and mean.

Fill every part of me with praise;
Let all my being speak
Of Thee and of Thy love, O Lord,
Poor though I be and weak.

So shalt Thou, Lord, from me, e'en me,
Receive the glory due;
And so shall I begin on earth
The song for ever new.

So shall no part of day or night
From sacredness be free;
But all my life, in every step,
Be fellowship with Thee.

Minister

The Blessing of God Almighty, the Father, the Son and the Holy
Ghost, be amongst you and remain with you – always. Amen.

APPENDIX VII

EPILOGUE

In the Light
by
The Rev. Leslie Timmins

Transmission: Sunday, 16 August 1959, 10.50–10.58 p.m. Fiat Lux (Dubois) played by Geoffrey Tristram, organ, from Christchurch Priory, Hampshire.

Timmins
'God is light, and in Him is no darkness at all . . . the darkness is passing away, and the true light already shineth.'

The Church where I work is in the middle of a big city, and it stands in a well-lit street.

No lamplighter comes down our road, because the lamps are like this.

The street is lit by those vapour lamps, and you'll have noticed that people look different under lamps like this. This girl spent some time choosing her make-up, and she looked just right when she left home for her date, but now her make-up looks wrong, and nothing matches. The boy friend looks a littler paler than usual too.

Of course it is true that light makes a lot of difference to the way we see things.

The beauty of the sunset you look at in a peaceful moment at the end of the day on holiday, depends so much on the angle of the sun, and the changing light as night falls.

The moon makes a path of light across the sea, and this is a lovely sight. But the same sea would look threatening and dark in the grey light of a storm.

So far we've been talking about the difference light makes to things and people outside. But lighting is on inside as well. I expect you have a light of some kind at this moment, even if it is only the light from your screen. This television studio has to be lit in a special way, so that you can see me. If the lighting was not well planned it could make a lot of difference to what you can see. And if we change the lighting in this studio so that I am lit only from behind it would make an enormous difference to the sort of picture you received on your screens.

See what I mean.

We've seen for ourselves how people and things look different when we look at them in different lights. But we also talk like this about ideas. Have you ever thought how often the word 'light' occurs in our conversation.

We say, for example, 'In the light of my experience'. We talk about a discovery shedding fresh light on a subject. These days we are learning so much so quickly about the world we live in, that our ideas are changing from day to day in the light of modern knowledge.

I speak every Saturday on Southsea Front to people in the open air, and the questions and answers are sometimes fast and furious. So many people are looking at things in different lights, that sometimes it seems impossible to know what is right and what is wrong.

Well then, does it make sense to talk about a true light, a clear light? Is there a kind of mental or spiritual light into which you can take ideas about life and examine them to see if they are true or false?

When I think about that I remember that there is a lot in the New Testament about light. In fact Jesus Christ said: 'I am the Light of the world'.

What did He mean?

I think He meant that if you will look at life with Him – through His eyes, so to speak, you will be able to see plainly what is right and what is wrong; what is true, and what is false.

Every day men and women are finding out that they need not walk in darkness, but that in the truth and presence of Jesus Christ, they have the power to choose what is good and true, and follow it.

It is my prayer tonight that you may have the Light of the world in your home, not only in the hours of darkness, while you sleep; but tomorrow, when daylight breaks, and you need to know what is valuable, and what is true.

God is light and in Him is no darkness at all.

The darkness is passing away and the true light already shineth.

APPENDIX VIII

A Killing on Canvas – TWW
Holy Week Programme 1964

TAM ratings compared with following programmes.

	Time	Rating	Followed by	Rating
Monday 23 March	11.13 p.m.	12	Hudsons Bay	11
Tuesday 24 March	11.20 p.m.	13	Close Down	
Wednesday 25 March	11.22 p.m.	14	This Wonderful World	9
Thursday 26 March	10.58 p.m.	22	University Challenge	21
Friday 27 March	11.05 p.m.	21	Joan Sutherland	10
Saturday 28 March	11.27 p.m.	15	Limelight	10

BIBLIOGRAPHY

The following books have been used in the preparation of this study, but are not directly quoted.

An excellent general Bibliography on radio and television is contained in *British Broadcasting: A Bibliography* which covers both BBC publications and a considerable number of ITA works.

GENERAL

Birtwhistle, A., *They Who Will Hear* (Epworth 1961)
Bogart, L., *The Age Of Television* (New York 1958)
Bonhoeffer, D., *Letters and Papers from Prison* (S.C.M. 1953)
Brandes, P. D., *Oral Communication* (Brown 1959)
British Broadcasting: A Bibliography (see above)
Brunner, H. and Barth, K., *Natural Theology* (1946)
Carnap, R., *Introduction to Semantics* (O.U.P. 1959)
Coase, R. H., *British Broadcasting: A Study in Monopoly* (BBC 1948)
Communist Party of Great Britain, *Literature as a Political Weapon* (C.P. 1955)
Coplestone, B. D., *Contemporary Philosophy* (Burns Oates 1956)
Dillistone, F. W., *Christianity and Communication* (Odhams 1956)
Flew, A. (ed.), *Essays on Logic and Language* (Blackwell 1951)
Gorham, M., *Broadcasting and Television since 1900* (1952)
Granada Lecture, Granada T.V., *Communication in the Modern World* (1959)
Hayakawa, S. I., *Language in Thought and Action* (1952)
Himmelweit (with Oppenheim and Vince), *Television and the Child* (1958)
Hodges, H. A., *Christianity and the Modern World View* (1949)
Hovland, *Communication and Persuasion* (1953)
Religion in Television. The Cambridge Consultation (ITA 1964)
Kraemar, H., *The Problem of Communication* (1956)
Niebuhr, R., *Beyond Tragedy* (1947)
Packard, V., *Hidden Persuaders* (1957)
Paulu, B., *British Broadcasting: Radio and Television in the United Kingdom* (1956)
Paulu, B., *British Broadcasting in Transition* (1961)
Read, D. H. C., *Communication of the Gospel* (1952)

Redfield, C. E., *Communication in Management* (1959)
Reith, J. C. W., *Broadcast over Britain* (1924)
Reith, J. C. W., *Into the Wind* (1949)
Sargant, W. W., *Battle for the Mind* (1957)
Schramm, W. L., *Responsibility in Mass Communication* (1957)
Sproxton, V., *Watching Films* (1948)
Swift, J., *Adventure in Vision: The first 25 years of Television* (1950)
Tillich, P., *Systematic Theology. Vol. I* (1951)
Tillich, P., *Shaking of the Foundations* (1949)
Unesco, *Television: A World Survey* (1953)
Van Buren, P., *The Secular Meaning of the Gospel* (1963)
Vidler, *Essays in Liberality* (1957)
Wilson, N. L., *Concept of Language* (1959)

INDEX